"Most people aren't willing to do the hard work it takes to make selling easy."

— Jeffrey Gitomer

Little Quotes
With BIG Meanings

"People don't like to be sold, but they love to buy."
Little Red Book of Selling by Jeffrey Gitomer

"The toughest answers in sales are
the ones you have to give yourself."
Little Red Book of Sales Answers by Jeffrey Gitomer

"All things being equal, people want to do business
with their friends. All things being not quite so equal,
people STILL want to do business with their friends."
Little Black Book of Connections by Jeffrey Gitomer

"The more you talk about and ask about THEM,
the more they will like you."
Little Green Book of Getting Your Way by Jeffrey Gitomer

"It's your thoughts behind the words you
speak that creates your attitude."
Little Gold Book of YES! Attitude by Jeffrey Gitomer

"When the customer is ready to buy,
their wallet is open. Empty it."
Little Platinum Book of Cha-Ching! by Jeffrey Gitomer

Jeffrey Gitomer's

SALES BIBLE

The ULTIMATE SALES RESOURCE

Including
The 10.5 COMMANDMENTS
of Sales Success

An Imprint of HarperCollins*Publishers*

THE SALES BIBLE, NEW EDITION

Published by HarperCollins Publishers, 10 East 53rd Street,
New York, NY, 10022

To order additional copies of this title, contact your local bookseller or call
704-333-1112.
The author may be contacted at the following address:
Buy Gitomer
310 Arlington Ave, Loft 329
Charlotte, NC 28203
Phone: 704-333-1112 Fax: 704-333-1011
Email: salesman@gitomer.com
Websites: www.gitomer.com, www.trainone.com

Edited by Jessica McDougall
Page design by Mike Wolff
Cover design by Josh Gitomer
Photography by Yanick Dery

Printed in China by R.R. Donnelley.

First Edition, May 2008

Library of Congress Cataloging-in-Publication Data

Gitomer, Jeffrey H.
  Jeffrey Gitomer's sales bible : the ultimate sales resource, including the
10.5 commandments of sales success / edited by Jessica McDougall . – New ed.
      p. cm.
  Rev. ed. of: The sales bible / Jeffrey Gitomer. Rev. ed. 2003.
  Includes index.
  ISBN 978-0-06-137940-6
    1. Selling–Study and teaching. I. Gitomer, Jeffrey H. Sales bible. II. Title. III.
Title: Sales bible : the ultimate sales resource, including the 10.5 commandments of
sales success.

  HF5438.2.G58 2008
  658.85–dc22

                                                                    2008004201

08 09 10   11   12   RRD   10 9 8 7 6 5 4 3 2 1

"I want to dedicate this book and issue a special 'thank you' to every prospect who ever told me no."

— *Jeffrey Gitomer*

I just made a sale!

You are my new customer.
Thank you for your business.
I appreciate your support and patronage.

With all the customers I serve through my speaking engagements, my weekly column, my e-mail magazine Sales Caffeine, *my online training business, and my writing, I have three goals:*

1. To help people.
2. To establish long-term relationships.
3. To have fun.

My goal in writing this book was to make it so helpful to you that you would tell (refer) ten of your co-workers and friends to buy one. Please let me know if I reach my goal with you.

Because of you, and all my other valued customers, I have the opportunity to do what I love to do.

Sell. Write. Speak. Teach.

Thank You!

Jeffrey Gitomer's
10.5 COMMANDMENTS
of Sales Success

THINK
1. The sale is in your head.

BELIEVE
2. Develop a four-part belief system that can't be penetrated.

ENGAGE
3. Develop rapport and personal engagement, or don't start the selling (buying) conversation.

DISCOVER
4. People buy for their reasons, not yours. Find out theirs first.

ASK
5. Ask the wrong questions – get the wrong answers.

OBSERVE
6. Your ability to observe must be as powerful as your ability to sell and your ability to listen.

DARE
7. Have the chutzpah to risk.

OWN
8. Know whose fault it is when the sale's not made.

EARN
9. Sell for the relationship, not the commission.

PROVE
10. One testimonial is worth one hundred sales pitches.

BECOME
10.5 You don't get great at selling in a day. You get great at selling day by day.

Jeffrey Gitomer's
10.5 Commandments
of Sales Success
The guiding principles of sales mastery

1. THINK. The sale is in your head.

The mindset by which you approach the sale will determine its outcome more than any other element of the selling process. Frame of mind and mindset. Friendly, smiley, enthusiastic, positive, confident, self-assured, likeable, and prepared beyond nervous. It's in your head, way before it's in your wallet.

Ever walk into a sales call thinking to yourself, "This is not a great appointment. The sale is probably *not* going to happen. And even though I'm kind of wasting my time – what the heck, I'll give it a shot." Sure you have. Every salesperson has had that happen 100 times.

You've also had the opposite happen. Walking in, thinking to yourself, "This is a great prospect. They need my stuff, they love my stuff, and they love me. The sale is in the bag."

Whichever way you walked into the call, YOU set the tone for the probable outcome. You also set the TONE for your attitude, your enthusiasm, and putting your belief system into motion.

The reality is: no salesperson on the planet makes every sale. But that doesn't mean that you should ever, ever, ever walk into a sale with anything less than a feeling of certainty that you will make the sale because the customer needs you, and that you are the best. Not the lowest price, but the best value.

Everybody has a different way of creating his or her mindset prior to a sale. Mine has always been getting thoroughly ready, which includes thinking of ways to immediately engage the customer, and listening to rock 'n' roll music until I enter their office. In my early days of selling, I listened to inspirational messages.

In the '70s, my two favorites were *The Strangest Secret* by Earl Nightingale and *The Psychology of Winning* by Denis Waitley. Both messages put me in a frame of mind to think about myself and pump myself up – when, in reality, I should have been thinking about my customer.

Over time I learned that being totally prepared in terms of the customer gave me that self-assurance, and listening to music made me feel good and gave me rhythm. Music and preparation created mindset. I was ready, happy, and certain I was gonna make the sale. That is still the case today.

ACTION: Before your next 100 sales appointments (yes, I said 100), write down what can happen that's good. What you expect the positive outcome to be. And at the end of the call write down what you could have done to make it better.

Thinking you will is dependent on your self-confidence. Your self-confidence is based on your preparation. Thinking you will, and letting your thoughts guide your success on a DAILY basis, will help you become **PROFICIENT**. This daily exercise will eventually become ingrained. It has for me, and I promise it will for you – but it must be DAILY.

Thought **MASTERY:** The secret to mastering your thought process, and believing you can and you will, was written by Jefferson Airplane, and the immortal lyric sung by Grace Slick: "Feed your head, feed your head, feed your head."

The next 9.5 commandments will lead you to the understanding of what it takes to create a relationship, and become successful – not just make a sale. They're the core principles – commandments – that will form the foundation of your sales success.

Each commandment is integrally linked to one another. All 10.5 must be practiced and followed in order for you to achieve the mastery and the results (the success and the money) that you're hoping for. But let me assure you that it's not only possible, it's probable that you can achieve – if you first think you can.

"I think I can. I think I can"
from The Little Engine That Could
by Watty Piper, 1930

2. BELIEVE. Develop a four-part belief system that can't be penetrated.

Believe in your company, your product, and yourself – or you won't sell.

Believe the customer is better off buying what you sell, and buying it from you. Know who the most important person in the world is… It's you!

Your belief system determines your fate. Not just in the selling process, but also in your career. Every seminar I've ever done, I talk about belief. Every book I've ever written talks about belief. And yet there are thousands, maybe millions, of salespeople who don't believe in anything but the money they might earn if they make a sale. As you look to succeed in your career, you have to believe in the company that you represent, and you have to believe that it's the best company in the marketplace offering or creating what you're trying to sell. You have to believe in their ethics. You have to believe in their ease of doing business. You have to believe in your co-workers. And you have to believe that the company will deliver what you sell in a manner that will create customer loyalty.

You have to believe that your products and services are not just the best in the marketplace, but that they're also the best value for the customer. You have to believe that you can differentiate yourself from your competitor, and that you can prove (through testimonials) that your product is what you say it is.

You've often heard it said that the first sale made is the salesperson - that the customer must buy you before they buy your company, your product, or your service. In order for this to take place, you have to believe in yourself. In order for that sale to be made, you must first sell yourself.

That self-belief will be evident in the passion that you create in your presentation as you try to transfer your message, engage the customer, and get them to buy from you. Your self-belief will be evident in your enthusiasm and in your self-confidence. And that self-belief begins with the mindset I spoke about in commandment one. Your belief is in your head, the same way the sale is in your head.

But the glue that binds the first three elements of belief (company, product, and self) is the belief that the customer is better off having purchased from you. That the customer's value, productivity, ease of use, profitability, and perceived win are greater with you and your products and services than any competitor could ever hope to offer.

ACTION: Write down the four why questions. WHY do I believe in my company? WHY do I believe in my products and services? WHY do I believe in myself? And… WHY do I believe my customer is better off having purchased from me?

To become belief **PROFICIENT**, every time you visit a customer, ask them why they believe in you, your company and your product. Then ask them why they buy from you?

To **MASTER** belief takes time. Developing your belief system is a combination of how you feel, how your company executes, and how your product performs. As your history of success broadens, your entire belief system deepens. The more your customer loves you, loves your product, and loves your company – the more you will love to sell it, and the more sales you will make. Your customers, the ones who love you, will help you deepen your belief system to a point that it becomes impenetrable.

3. ENGAGE. Develop rapport and personal engagement, or don't start the selling (buying) conversation.

Use the principle of leaning forward. Get the prospect to be interested in what you have to say. Let the dog chase you. Engage with questions and try to make them smile, make a friend, establish some rapport, and, if at all possible, find the LINK.

The customer is making a judgment on you from the moment you enter the door and begin the selling process. The old sales adage says, "All things being equal, people want to do business with their friends. All things being not quite so equal, people STILL want to do business with their friends." Rapport and engagement begins in a relaxed atmosphere between or among friendly people. You cannot control how friendly the other guy will be. But you have 100% control over yourself. When you walk in the door, or the meeting starts, it's likely that you will talk first. Your words set the tone and the atmosphere for whatever is to follow. If you talk about the weather, if you talk about the news, if you talk about your flat tire or your problems – you will lose respect, you will lose all chances for rapport, and you will lose the sale. Miserably.

And it's most likely that you will leave the sale blaming its loss on everyone except the person who lost it. That would be you.

I begin conversations, whether in person or on the phone, asking people where they live or where they grew up. Because I'm well traveled, it's likely that I will have something to say or even something in common with where they live or where they grew up.

I ask this question because it's engaging (people like to talk about themselves), and I ask this question because it's non-threatening, and it's non-salesy. It gets the conversation going in an easy and relaxed manner. Once I feel that I have some kind of initial rapport, I might ask, "How did you land here?" or "What made you decide to embark on this career?"

Now I'm a little more personal, but still not that personal. I'm not asking about family, religion, or politics. If they bring up family, I'm more than eager to talk about it. If they bring up religion or politics, I try to get out of that conversation in under one sentence. My personal rule of sales is very simple. I don't start any kind of sales conversation until I am certain that they are ready and willing. Ready to listen, and willing to receive my message.

PLEASE NOTE: The worst thing you can do is begin your meeting with your background, your company's background, or your product. If it's a big meeting, the likelihood is that your prospective customer already knows about your company, already knows about your product – and has probably Googled you (the same way you have Googled them).

It's amazing to me how many salespeople think that they are the only ones doing research before a sale. Most companies do twice as much research before they buy as a salesperson ever does before they sell.

The principle of leaning forward is most easily defined in boxing. During the fight, boxers chase each other all over the ring. Jabbing and throwing punches. But occasionally, one boxer is leaning forward as the other is throwing a punch. The term used is "walking into a punch." And the opponent immediately falls to the ground. Out cold. Your job, in establishing rapport, is to get the customer leaning forward with a pen so that when you slide the contract underneath it, he or she is ready to sign.

ACTION: Think about your last few sales. Write down how the sale began. Was it friendly? Did you feel comfortable when you began the sales portion of the meeting? Begin each sales call or phone call with informal, but MEANINGFUL, dialogue.

PROFICIENCY: Keep a one-sentence log of how you begin each appointment. I'll bet the appointments that have turned into sales are the ones where great rapport – even common ground – was established.

MASTER: You master personal engagement and rapport when you find common ground and laugh together EVERY TIME you make a call or have an appointment. The measure of this is not just making sales, it's creating relationships and friendships that end in multiple sales and referrals.

4. DISCOVER. People buy for their reasons, not yours. Find out theirs first.

This commandment could also read, **People don't like to be sold, but they LOVE to buy®.** The nuance of sales (that most people COMPLETELY overlook) is finding out WHY people buy. "Why they buy" is more valuable than "how to sell." Establishing their "why" is the basis of determining their true need(s). Their buying motive (their reasons for buying) is one billion times more important to the sale than your selling skills. Know "what you sell" in terms of the customer's need to buy – not in terms of your need to sell. They want to know how they can produce, profit, and succeed – not a bunch of crap about you.

People don't care what you do, unless they perceive it helps them. The way you explain your business and product determines the buying interest you create – say it in terms of the prospect, not in terms of you.

The best part about finding your customer's "reasons for buying" is that it will completely differentiate you from all your competitors trying to SELL.

Below are some points to consider as you seek to discover the insight that will create both urgency and orders. Here's why they buy:

Their **MOTIVE** for buying will get you to the heart of the sale and their desire to take action. You determine motive by asking questions about past history, experience, wisdom, ownership, and use.

Their **STORY** will begin to unfold as you ask motive-based questions. When you ask about their experience, a story will follow. Their story will contain major clues about likes and dislikes and how to establish a real relationship.

Their **PAST EXPERIENCES** will lead to stories both good and bad. Your job is to listen with the intent to understand, never interrupt, and at the end of the story *ask more questions.* The more questions you ask, the more information you will uncover about the next two motives.

Their **EXPERTISE** has been acquired from their past experience. Your job is to find out how much of an expert they are so that you don't look like a fool trying to be an expert if the customer is more of an expert that you are.

Their **WISDOM** is the final frontier of your questioning about their motives and their past experiences. Asking them what they've learned and asking them how they applied their knowledge will lead you to their wisdom. When you can get to wisdom, it means you have established rock-solid rapport.

Their **NEED** will also tell you their urgency to buy, if you're able to uncover how they will use and profit from what it is you're selling as opposed to what they're currently doing, or what they're currently using.

Their **WANT** is the emotional part of the selling process. The more they want it, the more they'll find a way to own it (just like you).

Their **DESIRE TO OWN** is similar to their need, but has more pride attached to it. The pride of ownership. Everyone wants to own the best. Not everyone is willing to pay for the best. The salesperson creates the difference.

Their **DESIRE TO WIN** enhances the emotion of wanting and needing if the customer believes they will gain a competitive advantage from buying your product or service.

Their **DESIRE TO SOLVE OR RESOLVE** present problems or situations in their company will also be a prime factor in purchasing urgency. The more they believe you are some form of salvation, the faster they will purchase.

Their **DESIRE TO RECOVER** is similar to solve or resolve but takes a longer time to decide. Recovery means some damage has been done, either physical, economic, or both. And even though they want to rebuild, their steps will be more cautious.

Their **PASSION** is their highest form of emotion. Sales are made emotionally then justified logically. The more you can uncover their passion, the more they will be willing to share their passion, and the more likely the sale will be made. Especially if they see that you are also a person of passion (belief).

Their **FEAR** is close to their passion. Fear of loss is greater than desire to gain. Yes, they want to beat the competition, but greater than that is their fear of losing to the competition. Once you understand this motive, you can proceed to greed…

Their **GREED** is loosely defined as their mental process of thinking about how much they will win by owning what you're selling. As you're talking, prospects are often doing what is known as "mental math," or figuring out their profit in advance. I always try to let customers calculate their own numbers. Much more powerful.

Their **VANITY** is important to them, even though it means pretty much nothing to you. When you try something on in a store, you look at yourself in the mirror and have a thought about how you appear. But when the clerk comes over and says, "You look GREAT in that!" immediately your vanity kicks in and you "hafta have it."

Their **DESIRE TO IMPRESS** carries the same weight as their vanity. Loosely referred to as *"keeping up with the Joneses,"* it's also expressed in some form of *"mine is bigger than yours"* or *"mine is better than yours."* I often think that America should be described as "Land of the Free, Home of the Brave, and my house is bigger than your house."

Their **PEACE OF MIND** normally comes from knowing they have what they want, even though they might not use it at this moment in time. Insurance is probably the best example of that. Investments may be a close second. The bottom line is the more peace of mind you can provide, the more likely you will be to convert your selling to their buying.

Their **DESIRED OUTCOME** is a critical element, maybe *the* critical element in their decision-making process. What do they believe will happen AFTER they take ownership? How will they produce? How will they benefit? How will they profit? Are they certain they will achieve their objectives? Are they confident in you providing the product or service that they're hoping for. NOTE WELL: If you get to a point where you have to sell, don't talk features and benefits; talk outcomes.

Their **UNSPOKEN RISK** is their hesitancy in moving forward. Whenever someone asks me how to create buyer urgency, I tell him or her to remove the risk that the buyer perceives but is not telling you. Those factors need to be explored with questions that normally begin with the word why.

Their **REASONS WHY** must be uncovered in order for you to get past risk. Why will they? Why won't they? Why are they hesitating? Why are they not telling me everything? The more "why" you can uncover, the more risk you can remove and the more you will get down to the real reason. Try to find more gentle ways of asking why. For example, "What makes you…" rather than "Why do you…."

ACTION: Take the list you have just read and see how many of the items you can relate to you and your selling situation. Then put the best ones into action starting with your next call or appointment. See what motives you can uncover.

PROFICIENCY: The moment you uncover what you believe to be a buying motive, write it down in a file called MOTIVES. After a few months, all of them will be evident. All of them will be revealed. Act on them. Modify your sales presentation to include the customer's reasons for buying.

MASTERY of buying motives takes time. And motives can change with the market. Your job is to know them all and know the related RISKS that go along with them. Mastery of motives comes when you have identified unspoken risks and removed them. Risk removal is not just mastery; it's sales mastery.

5. ASK. Ask the wrong questions – get the wrong answers.

FACT: Questions are the heart of the sale.

FACT: Questions convert the selling process to a buying process.

FACT: Questions uncover facts and motives for buying.

FACT: Most of what is written about asking questions is wrong – and I hope that's what your competition is using to learn questioning.

Develop and ask questions that make the prospect think about themselves, and answer in terms of you. Make them evaluate new information. Get them to give you answers in the form of information about themselves in terms of how they use, or what they think about, your product or service.

Your questions will reveal what they consider the value and benefit of ownership. BUT THE QUESTIONS MUST BE INTELLIGENT. And they must be different from the ones your competition asks, or you will be compared (unfavorably) to them. And worse, your prospect will become bored and disengaged.

Ask for their opinion often. Not only does it give you the prospect's perspective (the only one that matters), but it's also a great test close.

And PLEASE NEVER ASK, "What's important to you?" Find out what's important by asking other questions.

Ask YOURSELF questions BEFORE you ask the customer or prospect questions.

If you don't know these answers, don't go on the call.
- What impacts their business?
- How did they do last year? Or how are they doing now?

- How would they profit more or produce more as a result of buying and using what you sell?
- What are their possible motives for buying?
- Who are you talking to? The decision maker or someone that has to call their daddy?
- What is their present urgency?
- What is their experience?

I hear and read "sales gurus" that tell you what NOT to do, like don't bring brochures or a sales pitch to the meeting – TOTAL B.S. They're telling you not to be prepared for all eventualities. If you bring questions and ideas, you can drag in the kitchen sink and no one will care.

I want your prospective customer to be IMPRESSED and ENGAGED by your questions. The rest will take care of itself.

ACTION: *On your next sales call:*
- Take ten GREAT questions.
- Take BACKGROUND information about them.
- Take VALUABLE ideas they can profit from.

Do that, ask the questions, create valuable dialogue, engage them, and the ultimate "take" will be yours: the order.

And it STARTS with asking.

PROFICIENCY: The way you question will determine the way you sell. Refine yours every week until their power is evident by the increase in your sales.

I have always identified **MASTERY** of asking questions as when the prospect says, "Great question. No one ever asked me that before."

There is more on asking questions inside the book, but I wanted you to know how important questions are in converting selling to buying.

6. OBSERVE. Your ability to observe must be as powerful as your ability to sell and your ability to listen.

Half the answers are there for you to see…if you're looking. Principle 12 in my *Little Red Book of Selling*, is "Antennas Up." It talks about being alert and open at all times so that when an apparent opportunity arises you can take advantage of it. "Antennas Up" is PART of your ability to observe.

Everyone (including me) has told you when you go into someone's office look around for clues, ideas, and conversation pieces. Trophies, pictures, and diplomas are there for the looking. But they're also there for the thinking. The key thought is, *can you relate?* Or better stated, *how can you relate?*

If someone has a bowling trophy and you're not a bowler, the best thing to do is keep quiet about it. But if someone has a Harley Davidson replica on his or her desk, and you are a Harley owner or enthusiast, then it's time to talk. Those are obvious observations, and appropriate actions.

I read a short book some time ago entitled *Obvious Adams: The Story of a Successful Businessman*. It has been reprinted, and it is listed on the "Jeffrey's Suggested Reading List" page on www.gitomer.com. It's a story about the power of observation and afterthought, as it links to personal and business success. Maybe your success. Read it and see for yourself (make sure you buy the original version).

Observing leads to understanding IF you're paying attention. Think about the way you observe things now. Are you glancing at them or paying attention to them? Are you thinking about them as you're looking? Does what you observe create thoughts for you? Does what you observe create ideas for you? Does what you observe inspire you? If the answer is yes to all of those elements, then you may possess the power of observation.

Merely being observant harnesses no power. Looking, thinking, generating ideas, and taking actions as a result of your observations is the power.

Observation also creates insight. It reveals the obvious things you might miss about something or someone.

The good news is most people are somewhere between non-observant and oblivious. This gives you an immediate advantage. It always makes me feel good when I see what others don't, or see something that creates new thought.

ACTION: Carry a small notepad and begin writing your observations as they occur. Don't just write what you see. Write the thoughts that strike you as a result of what you see. Your reaction to what you see. And maybe your ideas from what you see.

To become **PROFICIENT** at observing, the habits of writing, thinking, and idea generating must be consistent. Daily. Ever alert. Ever paying attention.

To **MASTER** observation takes both daily practice and self-discipline. Sometimes at dinner, a friend or a customer will ask why I am not drinking. I respond, "Because I'm a writer and a thinker." Oh, I'll have a glass of wine every once in a while. But not two glasses. It would ruin my power of observation and my ability to discern what I see. You have to choose between being a drinker or a thinker.

Here's a fun exercise... Buy *The Adventures of Sherlock Holmes* DVDs with all the episodes and the original characters – Basil Rathbone and Nigel Bruce. Sherlock Holmes is the ESSENCE of observing and thinking – aka deducing. "Brilliant Holmes!" "Elementary, my dear Watson," the dialogue goes. Watch them all – they are entertaining, informative, and instructional.

7. DARE. Have the chutzpah to risk.

Chutzpah is loosely translated into English as guts, gumption, non-conformist, moxie, and throw in some gonads. It's a word used to admire the risk taking, or the bravado of someone. "He has chutzpah," is said when speaking about the prowess or accomplishment of another – in a positive way.

What is your risk factor? How willing are you to take risk in order to succeed?

The word risk has to be preceded with the words "tolerance for," or the words "willing to take a." How willing you are to risk and your tolerance for risk will determine whether you're willing to take the risk, or accept the risk.

Your personal risk might be buying a home or investing in stock. Your sales risk might be a humorous voicemail, a creative follow up, an out-of-the-ordinary proposal, or even asking for the sale when you're not sure what the answer will be. Risking and selling are synonymous words.

The quote I've most often used is one that's akin to, "No risk, no reward." I say, "No risk, no nothing." The reason I say it is that it provides insight into what every salesperson must accept as the basis for a career in sales. It's a risk, and you have to be willing to take risks to earn the rewards.

You often hear people say that they wouldn't or couldn't go into sales. The reason is they can't tolerate the risk involved. The uncertainty. The unknown. Or, perhaps more fundamental, they can't handle the challenge.

The reason I use the word chutzpah is because it more clearly defines the risking process for a person, and in a positive way. In a word it says *go for it*. Wait, that's three words. But you get the idea. It's walking out to the end of a diving board, looking down at the water ten meters below, and not simply having the courage to dive in, but having the chutzpah to yell to everyone around you, "Hey, watch this dive! It's my first one ever off a 10-meter board." NOTE WELL: If you've prepared well off the 5-meter board, there's a chance you could nail it. But, in any event, everyone will applaud your courage. Applaud your chutzpah.

ACTION: Every day is "chutzpah day" in selling. Whether it's cold calls, face-to-face appointments, lowering sales barriers, negotiating price, making a follow up, or asking for the sale – every day takes courage and application. Courage and action. Risk, and the chutzpah to take it.

Start Small. Take a few low-level risks to get in the groove. A few cold calls. Not just trying to get past the gatekeeper, but the chutzpah to get through to the decision maker, and ask for a sale. Try it.

Great News: Success breeds success, AND the confidence to do more. Risk more. Asking for the sale and making it leads to asking for more sales.

More Great News: This book is FULL of ideas that require the guts to try them. The more you try, the more you'll succeed.

PROFICIENCY REALITY: When you fail a few times, or get rejected a few times, it makes you call on your character, your reserve, your resolve – your *chutzpah* – to try again, just a little smarter, just a little harder, and succeed.

THE ONLY WAY TO MASTERY: Try an idea, a strategy, a sales idea. Try something new every day. Dare yourself to succeed.

8. OWN. Know whose fault it is when the sale's not made.

If they turn you down because of "price," whose fault is that? If they don't return your phone call, whose fault is that? If they decided to buy from the competition, whose fault is that? *Yours* – you couldn't get the prospect to lean forward.

IMPORTANT NOTE: Don't *blame* yourself – Take *responsibility* for it. Learn from it. And then do something about it!

Blame is easy to issue and spread, difficult (sometimes impossible) to accept.

Every time something goes wrong, or does not go your way in the selling process, the first thing you do is talk about why it's someone else's fault. They wouldn't return your phone call, they wouldn't make an appointment with you, they took a lower bid, they selected your competitor after they told you they were going to select you, your company provided lousy service, someone else didn't do their job properly, you'll even blame your car, or traffic, or the weather if you're late for an appointment.

These small blaming incidents create a pattern in your communication process that's not only negative; it's destructive. Self-destructive. I would love to have a nickel, even a penny, for every salesperson who has blamed something or someone when something goes wrong.

Instead of blaming, why don't you try thinking? And after thinking, try writing.

Think about what you could have done about the thing or person you're blaming? Could you have prevented it? Can you prevent it next time? What could you have said different that might have created a different outcome? Then think about what you can say right now about the thing or the person that you're blaming. How can you reconstruct the blame into a statement of responsibility?

For example, instead of saying "The guy didn't' return my call." Maybe you should say, "If I'd left a more creative voicemail, maybe the guy would have called me back," or "If my voicemail had value and purpose, maybe the guy would have called me back." The reversal of blame toward others is not to blame yourself. Rather, it's to take responsibility for what happened, and create a lesson from it so that blame becomes responsibility, becomes an idea or a new strategy, and ultimately becomes a sale.

Blame should only occur once. Statements like, "Hardly anyone ever returns my calls," or "I can't get any appointments," require a makeover. An extreme sales makeover. People are returning calls. People are making appointments. They're just not returning your calls or making appointments with you. And that's not just reality; it's opportunity.

ACTION: After blame converts to responsibility, ask yourself the question, *What can I do to prevent the situation from occurring next time?* This requires an idea session – a creativity session, or even a discovery session *with customers* who DO call you back, or DO make appointments with you – to find out why, and create new methodology.

PROFICIENCY: Use the lessons you learned from customers. And use their reasons, their "why," to create better approaches and methods.

MASTERY: Create regular meetings with customers. Get them one-on-one or with each other (especially if they are candidates to do business with each other), and create "value dialogue" to ensure their loyalty, and your continued understanding as to why they love you.

PERSONAL NOTE: I prefer to use the word methodology or strategy rather than idea. Idea is for the moment. Methodology and strategy are for the long term. Idea seems manipulative. Methodology and strategy are more relationship-oriented. In sales there is no fault. In sales there is no blame. There is accepting responsibility and capturing the immediate and the long-term opportunity that responsibility presents.

9. EARN. Sell for the relationship, not the commission.

If you make a sale, you can earn a commission. If you make a friend, you can earn a fortune. In sales you don't make money – you *earn* money. If you sell to help the customer, rather than meet your quota, you will set every sales record in the company. Help them build, win, produce, and profit – and you will earn the sale. Earning will also lead you to loyal customers who refer you to others, and are willing to give testimonials as to your value.

Most salespeople use the word "make" or "get." I don't. I use the words "work hard for" and "earn." I don't believe you make a sale. I believe you earn a sale. I don't believe you make a commission. I believe you work hard for and earn a commission. I don't believe you ask for a referral. I believe you earn a referral. The same with a testimonial.

Relationships do not happen in one or two sales calls. But what you say in one or two sales calls, or what you do in one or two sales calls, sets the foundation and the groundwork that makes a relationship possible. Your initial friendliness, your initial enthusiasm, your preparedness (especially with points of value for the customer), and your character creates an opportunity for a relationship to blossom, or not.

Sales quotas hamper relationship building. And while I know that's a broad statement, and some people might even disagree with it, I challenge you to think about this: If it's near the end of a month, or the end of a quarter, and you haven't made your goal or quota, the first thing that gets thrown out the window is relationship.

It's almost as stupid as companies reacting to a downturn in sales by cutting their marketing budgets and their training budgets. In both instances, efforts should be doubled rather than reduced.

If you had relationships, loyal customers, and a full pipeline, sales would be predictable. But if your pipeline is low or empty and you only have one or two good prospects at the end of a sales period and you "gotta make the sale," it becomes a battle of your need versus the customer's need. It's also your need versus the customer's perception of you.

If they perceive you as "needing it" they will back off. The smell of insincerity is one that reeks from panic and manipulation.

ACTION: Look at your "numbers" and see what you are required to produce. Now go back and look at your last ten sales.

PROFICIENCY: Call your ten best customers and schedule a breakfast or lunch. During the lunch, ask them how they define relationship. Ask them what is the BEST thing about doing business with you.

MASTERY: Once you are armed with the customer's definition of what makes a relationship, it's time to apply those master principles to everyone.

HERE'S THE REALITY: The harder you work to build relationships, the more you will earn loyal customers and the easier sales will become. Most salespeople will not do the hard work that it takes to make selling easy.

10. PROVE. One testimonial is worth one hundred sales pitches.

It's real proof of who you are and what you do. Testimonials can overcome objections one million times better than the best salesperson in the world. Video testimonials. What better proof have you got? What better answer could you give? When you get the right testimonials, you can walk in and say – "Here, watch this!" Testimonials sell where salespeople can't.

In every seminar, I ask my audience, "How many of you use video testimonials as an integral part of your selling process?" Almost no hands go up. I ask, "How many of you have video testimonials on your website?" Almost no hands go up. I ask, "How many of you include video testimonials with your proposals to prove the points that you're claiming?" Almost no hands go up. Then I ask, "How many of you think video testimonials would help you make a sale?" Almost every hand goes up.

I don't get it. They'll help you make a sale but you don't use them. Oh, I know why. It takes work. Or, you're waiting for someone else (marketing department) to do the work. You know marketing. They're the people who give you a deck of slides that don't work. Why are you waiting?

Video testimonials can be used in an ad campaign, on the web, with proposals, in your presentation, and to close a sale.

Testimonials are proof that you are who you say you are, and that your product or service will perform the way you say it will perform. Video testimonials are sales support, and if used properly a sales weapon of mass production.

ACTION: Get a video camera. (You probably already have one.) Call your five best customers. Tell them you'd like to come over. Bring lunch. And film them for a few minutes on why they choose you and why they choose your product or service. Do one per week. Make the testimonials specific. Have your customers talk about topics like price versus value, increase of productivity, switching from a competitor to you. Or some specific accolade that your company earns daily like speed of response, or the ability of your service people. Once you've collected all five video clips, use editing software to make the video pop. Keep the final product under five minutes. Then go out and try it a few times. It may be awkward at first, but once you realize its power, it will become an integral part of your selling process.

PROFICIENCY in testimonials comes from using the testimonials in multiple ways. Not just taking them with you on sales calls, but also using them on the Internet, or to create an ad campaign. Finding new ways to use testimonials will not only increase your sales, but it will also increase your belief in your company and your product and increase internal morale.

MASTERY of testimonials comes from making them more professional, making them more specific, and using them in a way that not only makes sales, but also eliminates competition. TRY THIS: The next time someone asks you for a proposal, tell the prospective customer that you will be providing video testimonials for every one of your claims inside the proposal – proof that what you say and what you're proposing is true – and request or demand that your prospective customer make your competitor do the same thing. This will not only create an ability for you to have an extreme competitive advantage, but it will also take the focus away from the issue of price, and place it where it belongs – on value.

10.5

BECOME.

"You don't get great at selling in a day. You get great at selling day by day."

— Jeffrey Gitomer

What did you do great today?

The daily dose. The daily achievement. The daily work toward a big goal. The big picture in daily actions. The small disciplined action.

I began my sales career at the age of seven. But I didn't learn my first sales idea until the age of 26. I never realized that there was a science of selling. No one ever talked about it in my home, even though it was an entrepreneurial home. I just assumed it was a combination of the gift of gab and chutzpah. I was wrong.

Once I began to learn sales and the selling process, I couldn't get enough. I read. I listened. I practiced. And I did it every day. And I still do it every day. In 1992, I added writing. In 1993, I added speaking. It took years to become successful at the science of selling. It took years to master the science of selling. And I still work at it diligently every day. And so must you if you're looking to succeed in a selling career.

Sales is not a matter of leads and appointments and closes. It's not even a matter of the quality of your product or your service response. Sales is a matter of who you are, what your attitude is, and how dedicated you are to personal excellence. It's how responsible you are for the actions that you take and how sincere you are about helping others win for themselves so that ultimately you can win for yourself. That's not a idea or a strategy. That's a philosophy.

As you read and re-read *The Sales Bible*, you will realize it's written in the voice of reality, from the voice of a salesman. There is no theory in this book. It has been written the same way I want you to become successful: day-by-day.

Yes, there are secrets. And yes, they don't seem too secretive once revealed. Things like "sell to help" and "be your best" and "give value first."

But the biggest non-secret salespeople fail to embrace is the consistent daily action towards an achievement.

Now that you are exposed to the 10.5 Commandments, your job is to become a scholar. Study them, put them into practice, and adapt them to your situation and style.

The 12.5 Values of a Sales Professional

1. The value of creating a difference between you and the competition.

The key is perceived value.

The biggest difference is the difference they perceive in YOU!

2. The value of knowing the difference between satisfied and loyal.

Satisfied customers buy anywhere. Loyal customer stay, fight for you, and refer.

Will they order again? Will they recommend you to others? That is the measure.

3. The value of your ability to speak and be compelling.

If your sales message is boring, they pass. If it's compelling, they want to buy.

Engage them with great questions and ideas.

4. The (value) of knowing everything or being too busy to learn.

Stay a student – every day. All the information you need to succeed already exists.

You may not be exposing yourself to it.

5. The value of establishing a friendly relationship.

All things being equal, people want to do business with their friends.

All things being not quite so equal, people still want to do business with their friends.

6. The value of your humor.

If you can make 'em laugh, you can make 'em buy. Study humor.

7. The value of your creativity.

Your key to being perceived as different lies in your creativity. Creativity can be learned.

8. The value of asking for the sale.

It's so simple, no one does it.

9. The value of your belief in yourself.

To make a sale, you gotta believe you work for the greatest company in the world,

You gotta believe you have the greatest products and services in the world,

You gotta believe you're the greatest person in the world. Three key words, *you gotta believe.*

10. The value of being prepared.

Most salespeople are half prepared.

They know everything about themselves, but they know nothing about their prospect.

11. The value of not whining and not blaming.

You may think you're the greatest – but if you whine and blame others, no one will like you, or respect you.

12. The value of an apple a day.

An hour of learning a day will make you a world class expert at anything in five years.

12.5 The value of a YES! Attitude.

Attitude is EVERYTHING – to you and your success.

You become what you think about.

Your attitude is at the core of every action you take.

Table of Contents

Practical sales information you can read daily
and use immediately.

*Read it from cover to cover.
Open it anywhere and learn
what you need for the moment.
Use it the minute you read it.*

Expanded Table of Contents

PART 2
PREPARING TO WOW! THE PROSPECT

The WOW! factor. Use it to land a big sale.
Are you using the WOW! factor?
Remember me? I'm a salesman. Just like all the others.

To sell or not to sell, that is the (power) question.
Can you close a sale in five questions?

You are now under my power (statement).

PART 3
PLEASE ALLOW ME TO INTRODUCE MYSELF

The 30-second personal commercial – how to write it.
The 30-second personal commercial – how to deliver it.
Got a referral? Here's the perfect approach.

"No Soliciting," the funniest sign in sales.
Get to the decision maker on a cold call.
Opening is as important as closing.
The cold call is fun. If you think it is.
Elements of a cold call that can make it hot.

PART 4
MAKING A GREAT PRESENTATION

Want to make the sale easier? Establish prospect rapport first.

12.5 ways to make the prospect confident enough to buy.

Where and when to establish buyer confidence.

Sales words and phrases to avoid at all costs. Honestly.

Physically involving the prospect = more sales.

Slide show stupidity. That's not you is it? Or is it?

PART 5 OBJECTIONS, CLOSING,
AND FOLLOW-UP. GETTING TO YES!

Will the real objection please stand up!

Real-world objections. Real-world solutions.

Objection Prevention.

The sale starts when the customer objects.

"I want to think about it."

"We spent our entire budget, honest."

"I want to check with two more suppliers."

"I want to buy, but the price is too high."

"I'm satisfied with my present source."

"I have to talk this over with my..."

"Call me back in six months."

What are the 19.5 early warning signals that the prospect is ready to buy?

When you answer a prospect's question, avoid two words — Yes and No.

How to ask a closing question.

The Puppy Dog Close.

Let the dog chase you.

Eat dessert first!

The most powerful close in the world is not a close.

PART 9 NETWORKING...
SUCCESS BY ASSOCIATION(S)

Networking — the challenge of making success contacts.

Networking 101. How to work a room.

Networking 102. How to milk a room.

Establishing rapport when working a room.

The Official Networking Game.

PART 10
PROPHETS AND PROFITS

The new breed of salesperson. A non-salesperson.

What's Bob Salvin got to do with it? Lots!

PART 11
UP YOUR INCOME!™

The pipeline of success.

PART 12
CAN I GET AN AMEN?!

Dads teach sales success without knowing it.

Commit yourself!

Afterword... When I grow up.

Your past and present hold the key to your future.

"Everyone wants to succeed at sales. Most people don't. It's not that they can't. It's just that they don't know how."

– Jeffrey Gitomer

THE SALES BIBLE

Part 1
The Rules. The Secrets. The Fun.

Genesis

Begin Now!

The Sales Bible is a success tool. A place where you can get insight about all facets of sales.

There are also rules. To succeed at sales you must:
- Know the rules
- Learn the rules
- Take ownership of the rules
- Live by the rules

The Book of Genesis reveals a story of the new way of sales, talks about a few of the basic rules, and presents a surefire way to achieve any rule, sales goal, or career goal…

Don't just read it.
Use it. Go for it.

"Whatever the mind can conceive and believe it can achieve."
Napoleon Hill

What's so new about a 15-year-old book?

Every year, my understanding of the selling process and the buying process increases, or should I say *takes a quantum leap*.

If you're reading this passage, you may have also read one of the books in my *Little Book* series. For that, I thank you. But for this, it's a challenge.

The Sales Bible started out as a definitive sales resource 15 years ago. Before e-mail. Before websites. And when cell phones were 50 cents a minute.

Times have changed.
So has *The Sales Bible*.

In this NEW EDITION, you will be upgraded to *Sales Bible 3.0*. Not just newer and better. More insightful. More actionable. And more compelling for you, the reader. Don't worry, I haven't left out the fun. In fact, I've added more of it. This new edition is laced with Randy Glasbergen's laugh-out-loud view of the sales profession and its realities.

I've spent years developing these strategies and ideas that you can implement in minutes, become proficient at in hours, and master in days.

This **new edition** of *The Sales Bible* is for you to read, enjoy, put into practice, and profit from. Now that you own it, take advantage of it.

"It'll never happen."

Where did this book come from?

As with most sales, it started when I got turned down. An article published about me and my sales skills in *The Charlotte Observer* in the spring of 1992 made my phone ring off the hook. I went running back to the paper to offer my services.

"I want to write a weekly article on sales," I trumpeted. Not only did they turn me down, they said, "It'll never happen." I said, "No, it'll never happen here."

That same morning – one hour later – I struck a deal with the *Charlotte Business Journal* to publish a weekly column on selling skills. I called it *Sales Moves*.

Next time someone tells you "never," remember that means "not for at least one hour."

My name is Jeffrey Gitomer and I'm a salesman. I don't have a Ph.D. I'm a college dropout. I don't live in an ivory tower. I live in Charlotte, North Carolina. I learned to sell in New Jersey and New York, where I grew up. I was in multilevel marketing when it was called pyramiding. I have cold called every office in downtown Charlotte, and I've cold called Fortune 500 company presidents and made the sale.

I've made $1 sales and I've made $1,000,000 sales. I'm a salesman who has been on the street for almost 30 years. Sometimes face up, sometimes face down. I love to sell.

Sales Moves first appeared in Charlotte's business journal on March 23, 1992. The column was an instant success. It soon found its way to Dallas, Atlanta, Denver, Princeton, and a number of other cities.

Mark Ethridge, publisher of the *Charlotte Business Journal*, Pulitzer Prize-Winning journalist, and my good friend and supporter, said that publishing *Sales Moves* was his most impactful marketing decision of 1992. WOW!

People began to call, and still do every day, from all over the country. Papers wanting to publish the column. Readers thanking me for helping them make sales. I found out that salespeople were hanging my weekly article on the wall in their offices. They were copying the column and passing it around. They were mailing it to friends and co-workers in other cities. They were using the column to lead sales meetings.

My daughter, Stacey, bought a car in Charlotte. Everyone in the dealership reads my article. When she got to the closing room (alone), they said, "We're giving you the best deal of the year because we don't want your dad to write anything bad about us."

The first day I wrote an article, I knew I would write a book. It was a natural progression. My good friend and mentor, Ty Boyd, suggested the same thing. Encouragement means a lot to a salesman. I'm grateful for his; I'm grateful for yours.

The material I use is mine. I'm drawing on my 40 years in selling experience, 16 of which have been in consulting. I've listened to thousands of hours of records, tapes, and CDs. I've read everything I could find. I've attended every seminar that time would permit. My mission is to learn as I teach. I seek to learn something new every day.

I'll continue to write my weekly column to provide you with info that you can use to make more sales out there in the trenches. Today. I know what you're up against. I know how hard you work. I know how frustrating it can be. I will help you.

I began the construction of the first edition of this book in August 1993. After countless late hours in the office, a week at Beech Mountain, NC, and a week at Hilton Head Island, SC, with my Macintosh, my ace critic, editor, and friend, Rod Smith, and my cat, Lito, I was done. I thought it would be a snap. 700 man-hours later – snap.

Here's *The NEW Sales Bible*, edited by my partner and alter ego, Jessica McDougall. It has plenty of what's new and keeps the tradition intact.

Thank you for being my customer.
I hope this book makes you as much money as it will me.

So, what's in it for you?

Your reward will be the achievement of the loftiest goals you've ever entertained for your sales career.

Your reward will be the recognition you'll get as a superior salesperson.

Your reward will be the personal satisfaction of being the best salesperson you believe you can be. And you did it yourself.

Your reward will be more sales.

I have designed this book to help you in every facet of your everyday sales tasks by providing practical, real-world solutions to your real-world selling situations and problems.

A real-world reference. A resource. A bible.

Before you begin this book, ask yourself the following questions:

- **How well do I think I sell?**

- **How do I practice my skills every day?**

- **How much time do I spend learning new sales skills?**

- **How many new ideas do I put into practice daily?**

- **How dedicated and committed to success am I?**

Sales is a discipline. Not a militaristic kind of discipline ("do it or peel potatoes"), but a personal dedication to achievement that can only occur when discipline is present. It's control that comes from within, not rules of law from without. Not the drudgery of discipline, the joy of it.

Discipline is the everyday process of focusing on what you want. And striving for it relentlessly until you get it.

I don't want to sound religious, but that's the closest comparative discipline there is. If you pray or meditate every day, that's the discipline, the ritual, you need to succeed at sales.

In sales, you get to make your own miracle.

As a salesperson, you're the most important person in the world of business!

Nothing happens in business until someone sells something.

You sell so that the factory can produce the orders, so that the product can be delivered, so that the administrative salaries can be paid, and so that the new computer system needed for the bean-counting department can be purchased.

Selling even occurs when you want the bank to loan you money or extend your line of credit. You must sell your banker or vendor on your ability to perform and repay.

8.5 ways to use this book…

Salespeople are constantly searching for new ideas.
Salespeople need a constant source of motivation.
Salespeople need immediate answers.
Salespeople are looking to make more sales… today.

Salespeople have lots of problems all at once. In the same day they cold call, follow-up with ten prospects, go to a networking event, make three presentations, send five letters, get turned down six times, and make one sale. That's a regular day! Salespeople need a dependable reference with real-world answers to their immediate questions, stumbling blocks, and challenges. They need *The Sales Bible*.

The Sales Bible is not a "method" of selling. It's a series of real-world observations, strategies, and philosophies that you can modify to your style of selling. You use what you need to make the sale today. You use what you need to prepare for the sale tomorrow. And you acquire the knowledge you need to achieve your sales goals.

The Sales Bible is a real-world resource. These lessons aren't a bunch of highbrow, Ph.D., clinical research. They're the result of 40 years of success and failure in some of the toughest selling environments the business world has to offer.

They're based on actual
experiences of mine that
I know work because
I worked 'em. They are
simple, pragmatic solutions,
and they make sense
where it counts…

In your sales environment.

They will help in your real world. Try a few and see.

Here's how you can use and benefit from this book:

1. As a resource. To expand and strengthen your knowledge and expertise in the selling process and daily sales challenges.

2. For a daily lesson. As part of your daily rededication to be the best.

3. In a study group. To grow and develop as a professional salesperson.

4. To lead a meeting. Most chapters are an ideal length to use as a guide for a sales training or brainstorming meeting.

5. To solve a problem. When you're out of ideas and need an answer now.

6. To prepare for a sale. To gain a competitive advantage.

7. To close a sale. The solutions and answers are all here.

8. In the heat of the battle. Take it with you as you work your sales day and reach for it as the doors begin to slam in your face, as the important contacts need to be made, and when that hot prospect won't return the voice-mail message you left for the third time.

8.5 Double your money. So many salespeople have unharnessed talent. I challenge you to double your income. I'm going to give you the tools to do it. It will be up to you to prove it to yourself. Can you develop the discipline needed to do it?

*"I won the door prize at the selling seminar.
It's a compass that always points to money!"*

HERE'S ONE GREAT WAY TO ABUSE THIS BOOK: As you read it, read with a yellow highlighter and a red pen. Highlight the areas that pertain to the knowledge you seek. Write your thoughts, your action plans, and your ideas in the margins.

HERE'S ONE GREAT WAY TO LEARN FROM THIS BOOK: For maximum benefit, use the information you read as soon as you can. Try it on a prospect or customer. As soon as you use it, you own it. One new idea per day is 220 new ideas per year. In five years, you'll have more than 1,000 ideas at your command. WOW!

Carry this book with you. Use it as a resource and a reference. Read a chapter at lunch. Discuss an idea with your co-workers. But most of all, use it to make sales. Lots of sales.

THE SPIRIT OF SALES. Each chapter has a quote at the top that's designed to capture the spirit and its content. Spirit plays a major role in *The Sales Bible*. The spirit in which the information is offered and the spirit in which it's received – and used. Each lesson stands on its own. Each lesson evolves to the next. Each lesson interacts with the others. Each lesson reflects the whole. Each lesson contributes to the whole.

Read the section titled "Post-It Note your way to achievement" found in *Genesis*. Use this method to chart your progress throughout this book. It will be good practice, and it will ensure that you get the maximum benefit.

Set goals for chapters you'll read each day. Set specific goals for enacting what you've learned. Set goals for improving your attitude. Set goals for having fun in your career. Then set goals for big sales.

Free GitXBit...Want reinforcement for the ideas and strategies contained in this book? I've created flashcards that you can carry with you on sales calls, to networking events, or to a trade show for quick reference under fire. The flashcards reinforce the principles of sales and will help you gain mastery in the selling process. For your printable copy, go to www.gitomer.com, register if you're a first-time visitor, and enter the word FLASHCARDS in the GitBit box.

The old way of selling doesn't work anymore – sort of.

It went out with leisure suits and bell-bottoms. You still wear clothing, just in a different fashion. The same in sales. You must change the way you sell in this decade, or you will not make enough sales to break even, much less to meet your goals and dreams.

The recession of the '90s forced a change in the sales process that will benefit the world of business forever. To succeed as a sales professional, you must be able to sell someone twice. Or sell to someone who will go out of his or her way to refer you to someone else.

The new way uses the old way. You must still be a master of every sales idea – just employ them in a different way. A friendly way. A sincere way. A way that emphasizes serving first and selling second. It always grates me when someone says 'selling is an art.' Baloney. Selling is a science. It is a response-triggered, repeatable set of words, phrases, and ideas that move the prospect to buy. Like science, it requires experimentation to determine what works best.

The new rules of the game are simple, and you can apply them today.

Your challenge is not just to use them, but to master them. Here are 7.5 to ponder, but there are hundreds in the pages that follow…

1. Say it (sell it) in terms of what the customer wants, needs, and understands. Not in terms of what you've got to offer.

2. Gather personal information. And learn how to use it.

3. Build friendships. People want to buy from friends, not salespeople.

4. Build a relationship shield that no competitor can pierce. My competitors call on my clients from time to time. My clients have actually given them my number and told the competitor to call me and get my opinion of their services. They say, "Call Jeffrey Gitomer and explain it to him. If he thinks it's okay, he'll tell us." Will your clients do that if your competitor calls them? What are you doing to ensure it?

5. Establish common ground. If you both like golf or have kids, you've got issues and topics in common that will draw the two of you closer.

6. Gain confidence. Once you motivate them to act, you'd better have built enough confidence to buy, or they'll buy from someone else.

7. Have fun and be funny. It ain't brain cancer, it's your career. *Have a great time*. If you can make 'em laugh, you can make 'em buy. Laughter is tacit approval. Tacit approval leads to contractual approval.

7.5 Never get caught selling. It makes me mad when a salesperson sounds like a salesperson. Learn the science and convert it to an art.

There are hundreds of other rules, guidelines, strategies, and ideas contained in these pages that are dedicated to the science of selling and why people buy. Your challenge is to learn to use them daily to succeed in the real world. Your world.

If you read one lesson in this book every day and practice it as soon as you read it, you will have more than 100 lessons and more than 1,050 ideas in less than six months.

Want to learn the best, easiest surefire way to sell everyone you meet? Read *Grimm's Fairy Tales*. You won't sell everyone. But you can sell more than you're selling now, much more. There is an easy way. And it's fun.

As you read *The Sales Bible*, gain new knowledge and implement it daily. Learning from the daily experience of its implementation leads to sales mastery. If you don't follow the process, sales will remain a mystery. You may not fail, but you won't succeed. Not the way you want to.

Selling is fun and selling is lucrative – but only if you're willing to get serious about your commitment to being the best you can be at it.

To succeed at selling, you must realize that there is not just one way to sell; there are thousands. You learn a little from everyone, combine it with your experience, and adapt it to your personality to develop your style.

There's one thing I have found after selling and studying sales for 40 years that is the absolute truth – the best salespeople are the ones with the best attitude, the best product knowledge, and who give the best service.

I have come to an understanding about sales and how sales are made. I came to that understanding after years of making and not making sales, after cold calling and getting hung up on, and after cold calling Fortune 500 presidents and making the sale. My objective is to share that understanding with you so that you can use it to make more sales. Lots more.

You will look at those Post-it Note goals
until you are sick of looking at them…
and then you'll begin to accomplish them.

Post-It Note your way
to achievement.

GOAL: I want to be a success.

CHALLENGE: Easier thought than done.

THOUGHT: Success means achieve goals.

WRONG THOUGHT: Many people are afraid of success.

REALITY: People aren't afraid of achieving success. They just don't know how to do it.

IDEA: Go purchase a pad of Post-it Notes, and you'll be on the path to success!

You have several goals you want to achieve, but they're not written down *in plain sight*. They just sit on a piece of paper in a drawer or pop up in your head every once in a while – only to be buried in a black hole of procrastination, excuses, and guilt.

TAKE HEART: I found a way to beat the system. Want to achieve your goals?

Here are the necessary tools for you to achieve the success that has eluded you thus far:

Post-It Notes   Bedroom Mirror
Bathroom Mirror Pen

And here's the tested and proven method:

1. Write down big ones. On 3X3 yellow Post-It Notes, write down your prime goals in short words. (Get funding for business. Win salesman of the year. New client: Wachovia Bank.)

2. Write down small ones. Use three more notes to write down your secondary goals in short words. (Read about attitude 15 minutes a day. Read book: Dale Carnegie. Organize desk. Build new closet.)

3. Put them in front of your face. Post them on your bathroom mirror, where you're forced to look at them – and yourself – every morning and every evening.

4. Say them aloud each time you look at them. Looking at *and* saying them double the affirmation.

5. Keeping looking and talking until you act. You will look at them until you're sick of looking at them. Then you'll begin to take action – achievement action – and accomplish them.

6. Seeing the note there every day makes you think about acting on it every day. Once you start acting, the note triggers a "What do I have to do today to keep the achievement on target?" The note forces you to act and achieve your goal.

By posting the goal in the bathroom, you are consciously reminded of your goals at least two times a day. From there your subconscious gets into the act, gnawing away at your soul until you are driven to take positive action. Achievement actions.

And when you get to the top of the mountain – when you achieve what you've been working for – at last you can say the magic words. Scream them – I DID IT! (Screaming positive things always feels wonderful.)

6.5 Revisit your success every day. Here comes the best part – after your goal is achieved, *take the Post-it Note off the bathroom mirror and triumphantly post it on your bedroom mirror.* Now, every day when you check out "how you look for the day," you also get to see your success.

Not only does it feel great, but you are able to set the tone for a successful day, every day, first thing in the morning by looking at (goal) success, remembering how good it felt, and thinking about what it took to do it. Plus – it gets you motivated to keep achieving more.

- **The program is simple.**
- **The program works.**
- **The results will change your attitude.**
- **The results will change your life.**
- **The results will change your outlook about your capability of success achievement.**

By the time you have your bedroom mirror full of achieved Post-it Note goals, you'll have enough money to go out and buy a bigger mirror – and the house to put it in.

Get your Post-It Note goal achiever starter kit. Want a preprinted pad of Post-it Notes to get started? I'd love to send you one in appreciation of your continued support and readership. **Send $1 to cover postage** to Buy Gitomer, 310 Arlington Ave., Loft 329, Charlotte, NC 28203.

"I print my goals on sticky notes and keep them close by so I can refer to them anytime during the day. My wife wrote this one about the toilet seat."

THE SALES BIBLE

Part 1
The Rules. The Secrets. The Fun.

The Book of Rules

"Rules are in every company for everyone to follow. Eh, except salespeople."
— Jeffrey Gitomer

Rules...
And the guidelines that turn them into sales.

How do you turn a prospect into a customer?

Let me count the ways. There are 39.5 ways.

Read them and you'll say, "Aha!"

Follow them and you'll say, "Thanks for the order."

Sales rule!

*Following the fundamental
rules of selling will lead to
sales success faster than any
high pressure sales idea.*

39.5 Rules of Sales Success

People aren't afraid of failure; they just don't know how to succeed.

In 1960, I met a college basketball coach on the court and asked him for his best, niftiest pointer. He took the ball, walked under the basket, and shot an easy lay-up. "See that shot?" he said gruffly. "Ninety-nine percent of all basketball games are won with that shot. Don't miss it." And he walked away. I felt cheated that day, but 20 years later, I realized it was the best sales lesson I ever got. Concentrate on the fundamentals; ninety-nine percent of all sales are achieved that way.

You are responsible for your own success (or failure). Winning at a career in sales is no exception. To ensure a win, you must take a proactive approach. Prevention of failure is an important part of that process. If you find yourself saying, *"I'm not cut out for sales," "I'm not pushy enough," "I hate cold calling," "I can't take the rejection," "My boss is a jerk,"* or *"My boss is a real jerk,"* you're heading down the wrong path.

Here are 39.5 recurring characteristics and traits of successful salespeople. How many of these apply to you? How many of these guidelines can you honestly say you follow? If you are serious about achieving sales success, I recommend you post this list someplace where you can see it every day. Read it and practice these principles until they become a way of life.

1. Establish and maintain a positive attitude. It's the first rule of life. Your commitment to a positive attitude will put you on an unstoppable path to success. If you doubt it, you don't have a positive attitude. A positive attitude is not just a thought process; it's a daily commitment. Get one!

2. Believe in yourself. If you don't think you can do it, who will? You control the most important tool in selling: your mind.

3. Set and achieve goals. Make a plan. Define and achieve specific long-term (what you want) and short-term (how you're going to get what you want) goals. Goals are the road map that will direct you to success.

4. Learn and execute the fundamentals of sales. Never stop learning how to sell. Read, listen to tapes, attend seminars, and practice what you've just learned. Learn something new every day and combine it with hands-on experience. Knowing the fundamentals gives you a choice in a sales call. Even in a relationship or partnership, sometimes an idea is needed.

5. Understand the customer and meet his or her needs. Question and listen to the prospect and uncover true needs. Don't prejudge prospects.

6. Sell to help. Don't be greedy because it will show. Sell to help customers; don't sell for commissions.

7. Establish long-term relationships. Be sincere and treat others the way you want to be treated. If you get to know your customer and concentrate on his best interest, you'll earn much more than a commission.

8. Believe in your company and product. Believe your product or service is the best and it will show. Your conviction is evident to a buyer and manifests itself in your sales numbers. If you don't believe in your product, your prospect won't either.

9. Be prepared. Your self-motivation and preparation are the lifeblood of your outreach. You must be eager and ready to sell, or you won't. Be ready to make the sale with a sales kit, sales tools, openers, questions, statements, and answers. Your creative preparation will determine your outcome.

10. Be sincere. If you are sincere about helping, it will show, and vice versa.

11. Qualify the buyer. Don't waste time with someone who can't decide.

12. Be on time for the appointment. Lateness says, "I don't respect your time." There is no excuse for lateness. If it can't be avoided, call before the appointed time, apologize, and continue with the sale.

13. Look professional. If you look sharp, it's a positive reflection on you, your company, and your product.

14. Establish rapport and buyer confidence. Get to know the prospect and his company; establish confidence early. Don't start your pitch until you do.

15. Use humor. It's the best tool for relationship sales I have found. Have fun at what you do. Laughing is tacit approval. Make the prospect laugh.

16. Master the total knowledge of your product. Know your product cold. Know how your product is used to benefit your customers. Total product knowledge gives you the mental freedom to concentrate on selling. You may not always use the knowledge in the sales presentation, but it gives you confidence to make the sale.

17. Sell benefits, not features. The customer doesn't want to know how it works as much as he wants to know how it will help him.

18. Tell the truth. Never be at a loss to remember what you said.

19. If you make a promise, keep it. The best way to turn a sale into a relationship is to deliver as promised. Failure to do what you say you're going to do, either for your company or your customer, is a disaster from which you may never recover. If you do it often, the word gets out about you.

20. Don't down the competition. If you have nothing nice to say, say nothing. This is a tempting rule to break. The sirens are sweetly singing. Set yourself apart with preparation and creativity – don't slam them.

21. Use testimonials. The strongest salesman on your team is a reference from a loyal customer. Testimonials are proof.

22. Listen for buying signals. The prospect will often tell you when he is ready to buy – if you're paying attention. Listening is as important as talking.

23. Anticipate objections. Rehearse answers to standard objections.

24. Get down to the real objection. Customers are not always truthful; they often won't tell you the true objection(s) at first.

25. Overcome barriers. This is a complex issue – it's not just an answer, it's an understanding of the situation. Listen to the prospect, and think in terms of solution. You must create an atmosphere of confidence and trust strong enough to cause (effect) a sale. The sale begins when the customer says no.

26. Ask for the sale. Sounds too simple, but it works.

27. When you ask a closing question, SHUT UP. The first rule of sales.

28. If you don't make the sale, make a firm appointment to return. If you don't make the next appointment when you're face-to-face, it may be a long, hard road to the next one. Make some form of sale each time you call.

29. Follow up, follow up, follow up. If it takes between five and ten exposures to a prospect before a sale is made, be prepared to do whatever it takes to get to the tenth meeting.

30. Redefine rejection. They're not rejecting you; they're just rejecting the offer you're making them.

31. Anticipate and be comfortable with change. A big part of sales is change. Change in products, tactics, and markets. Roll with it to succeed. Fight it and fail.

32. Follow rules. Salespeople often think rules are made for others. Think they're not for you? Think again. Broken rules will only get you fired.

33. Get along with others (co-workers and customers). Sales is never a solo effort. Team up with your co-workers and partner with your customers.

34. Understand that hard work makes luck. Take a close look at the people you think are lucky. Either they or someone in their family put in years of hard work to create that luck. You can get just as lucky.

35. Don't blame others when the fault (or responsibility) is yours. Accepting responsibility is the fulcrum point for succeeding at anything. Doing something about it is the criterion. Execution is the reward (not the money – money is just the by-product of perfect execution).

36. Harness the power of persistence. Are you willing to take *no* for an answer and just accept it without a fight? Can you take *no* as a challenge instead of a rejection? Are you willing to persist through the five to ten exposures it takes to make the sale? If you can, then you have begun to understand the power.

37. Find your success formula through numbers. Determine how many leads, calls, proposals, appointments, presentations, and follow-ups it takes to get to the sale. And then follow the formula.

38. Do it passionately. Do it the best it's ever been done.

39. Be memorable. In a creative way. In a positive way. In a professional way. What will they say about you when you leave? You always create a memory. Sometimes dim, sometimes bright. Sometimes positive, sometimes not. You choose (and are responsible for) the memory you leave.

39.5 Have fun! It's the most important of them all. You will succeed far greater at something you love to do. And doing something you enjoy will also bring joy to others. Happiness is contagious.

Not following the 39.5 Rules of Sales Success leads to slow but sure failure. It doesn't happen all at once – there are degrees of failing.

Here are 4.5 of them. What degree are you?

1. **Failing to do your best.**

2. **Failing to learn the science of selling.**

3. **Failing to accept responsibility.**

4. **Failing to meet quota or pre-set goals.**

4.5 **Failing to have a positive attitude.**

Success is a level of performance and a self-confidence brought about by winning experiences. Failure is not about insecurity. It's about lack of execution. There's no such thing as a total failure.

Zig Ziglar has an answer: "Failure is an event, not a person." Vince Lombardi said it better: "The will to win is nothing without the will to prepare to win."

The guy who wins the 100-meter dash in the Olympics does it in just under 10 seconds, every time. Ten seconds isn't too long to run in a race, but how long did it take him to prepare to run it? Do you have the same will to win? I hope so.

"This pays a lot better than selling lemonade!"

Sales Success Formula…

AHA!

Attitude – Humor – Action

This is a combination of elements I have found to be effective for sales achievement. It's simple on the surface and even simpler in practice. Each element contributes to the whole and is vitally linked to the other two. They are useful by themselves, but together they make sales magic.

Here's how it breaks down:

ATTITUDE. Your positive mental attitude is your driving force to success in every endeavor of your life. Positive attitude is not just a thought process; it's a discipline and a commitment. Each day you wake to a rededication to being positive, thinking positive, and speaking positive. It's not something that comes and goes. It's all-consuming. It makes you feel good all the time on the inside, no matter what the circumstance is on the outside.

HUMOR. It's not just being funny. It's how you see things. Humor is a perspective for effective living and a successful career in sales. It's your sense of humor AND your ability to find and create humor. Making others laugh and feel good in your presence. Making others smile. Hearing, "I like talking to you," "You make me laugh," or "You just made my day." That's what humor does. It makes others look forward to talking to you instead of ducking your call. It's medicine. Sales medicine.

ACTION. Walking your talk. Waking up in the morning to a clearly defined set of goals. Having a daily agenda that you're prepared for. Making the last call. Following your own game plan for success. Doing more than anyone else you know. Doing enough to make yourself proud.

The combination of these three elements will provide the pathway to your success.

"I challenge you to master each element, then combine them in your own way to suit your own personality.

The monetary results will astound you, but the personal reward is way beyond money."

Follow them to the letter and you'll say ...

"AHA!"

THE SALES BIBLE

Part 1
The Rules. The Secrets. The Fun.

The Book of Secrets

1.3

The Rules. The Secrets. The Fun.

Secrets…

Listen. (Tu-da-lu)
Do you want to know
a secret?

In order to master a trade,
you must know its secrets.

Knowledge of sales secrets
can save you years of
frustration and wasted
effort.

Learn these sales secrets
and … master the mystery.

50% of success is believing you can.
Simply put, you become what you think about.

Why do salespeople fail?

Because they think they will.

Do you have a positive attitude? Everyone will say yes, but less than 1 in 1,000 actually do! One-tenth of 1%. Are you really in that small percentile? All you have to do is pass this simple test.

Yes No

☐ ☐   I watch the news at least one hour per day.

☐ ☐   I read the paper every day.

☐ ☐   I read a news magazine every week.

☐ ☐   I sometimes have a bad day, all day.

☐ ☐   My job is a drag.

☐ ☐   I get angry for an hour or more.

☐ ☐   I talk to and commiserate with negative people.

☐ ☐   I look to blame others when something goes wrong.

☐ ☐   When something goes wrong or bad, I tell others.

☐ ☐   I get angry at my spouse and don't talk for more than four hours.

☐ ☐   I bring personal problems to work and discuss them.

☐ ☐   I expect and plan for the worst.

☐ ☐   I'm affected by bad weather (too cold, too hot, rain) enough to talk about it.

0-2 YES answers: You have a positive attitude.
3-6 YES answers: You have a negative attitude.
7 or more YES answers: You have a problem attitude. Serious problem.

More than 4 YES answers? Go out and invest in the books, CDs, and courses of Dale Carnegie, Norman Vincent Peale, W.Clement Stone, Napoleon Hill, Earl Nightingale, and Denis Waitley. These people tell you *how you can*, not why you can't.

THE PLOT THICKENS. Several national tests have revealed the following startling statistics about why salespeople fail:

- **15% Improper training – both product and sales skills.**
- **20% Poor verbal and written communication skills.**
- **15% Poor or problematic boss or management.**
- **50% Attitude.**

Sounds almost impossible, doesn't it? Salespeople (or anyone else) could succeed 50% more if they just change the way they think. Earl Nightingale in his legendary recording, *The Strangest Secret*, reveals the secret of a positive attitude: "We become what we think about." But it's a dedicated discipline that must be practiced. Every day.

Want to begin to change your attitude? It will miraculously affect your success (and income). Live these thoughts and exercises:

- **When something goes wrong, remember it's no one's fault but yours.**
- **You always have (and have had) a choice.**
- **If you think it's okay, it is. If you think it's not okay, it's not.**
- **Ignore the junk news. Work on a worthwhile project, make a plan, or do something to enhance your life.**
- **For one year, read only positive books and material.**
- **When you face an obstacle or something goes wrong, look for the opportunity.**
- **Listen to attitude tapes, attend seminars, and take courses.**
- **Ignore people who tell you that "You can't" or try to discourage you.**
- **Check your language. Is it half full or half empty? Partly cloudy or partly sunny? Avoid *why, can't,* and *won't.***
- **Say why you like things, people, job, and family. Not why you don't.**
- **Help others without expectation or measuring (keeping score). If you say, "I'm not because he's not," who loses? If you say, "Why should I, when he only..." who loses?**
- **How long do you stay in a bad mood? If more than five minutes, something's wrong.**
- **Count your blessings every day.**

If you take the hour a day that you currently waste watching the news and convert it into positive action or learning for yourself, your business, or your family, at the end of one year you will have captured more than 15 full 24-hour days. Which will help your success more – 15 days a year watching the news or 15 days a year building your future? You have a choice.

"When Vince Lombardi said, 'Winning isn't everything, it's the only thing,' he should have substituted the word *attitude* for *winning* to get closer to the truth."

— *Jeffrey Gitomer*

Are you born to sell?
No, you learn to earn!

You've heard it; you've probably said it: "That guy's a born salesman."
Baloney! That is one of the biggest fallacies in sales. Selling is a science.
An acquired skill. The salesperson who you thought was born to sell
painstakingly developed the traits and characteristics to do so, then went
about learning and applying the science of selling.

Take this personal inventory test. These are 21 traits and characteristics of
great salespeople. How many do you have? (IMPORTANT NOTE: There is
a middle ground between *yes* and *no* for salespeople called "working on
it." You're better off marking it *no* until you achieve that characteristic.)

Yes	No	
❐	❐	I have set my goals in writing.
❐	❐	I have good self-discipline.
❐	❐	I am self-motivated.
❐	❐	I want to be more knowledgeable.
❐	❐	I want to build relationships.
❐	❐	I am self-confident.
❐	❐	I like myself.
❐	❐	I love people.
❐	❐	I love a challenge.
❐	❐	I love to win.
❐	❐	I can accept rejection with a positive attitude.
❐	❐	I can handle the details.
❐	❐	I am loyal.
❐	❐	I am enthusiastic.
❐	❐	I am observant.
❐	❐	I am a good listener.

Yes	No	
❐	❐	I am perceptive.
❐	❐	I am a skillful communicator.
❐	❐	I am a hard worker.
❐	❐	I want to be financially secure.
❐	❐	I am persistent.

Answer over 15 with an HONEST yes and you've got what it takes. Between 10 and 14, it could go either way (better chance if you answered yes to knowledge, enthusiasm, self-confident, perceptive, self-motivated, and persistent). Under 10, don't do it even if it would mean world peace, an end to disease, and helping the space program.

Note Well: None of the above statements said anything about closing sales or overcoming objections The science of selling can be learned and applied easily if you embody the above traits. All you have to do is believe you can do it, commit yourself to doing it, and live up to your commitment.

"We're not ordinary sales people anymore!
From now on we're Deal Man, Dollar Boy, and
The Amazing Madame Cold Call!"

What's wrong with this sale?
It's you, Bubba!

In 25 years (has it been that long?) of sales training, I've never had a salesperson come up to me and say, "Jeffrey, I didn't make the sale and it was all my fault."

Salespeople make the fatal mistake of blaming other things, circumstances, and people for their own inability to create a buying atmosphere. And that mistake has double jeopardy. One, you're blaming the wrong party, and two, you issue blame instead of taking responsibility. You fail to see the urgent need for more self-improvement training.

I have identified 12.5 fatal flaws of selling. Real reasons why salespeople fail to make the sale. Painful as this exercise may be, why don't you rate yourself instead of just reading them. And for your maximum enjoyment and benefit, a one sentence "flawless" remedy or suggestion follows each flaw.

Here are the fatal flaws. How many of them are fatal to you? Go get a red pen and as you read, put an "F" by the flaws you may want to improve.

1. Being a puppy, puppet or pawn. Salespeople are too happy to oblige without getting a commitment or adding an idea or thought. *Flawless:* When you send a brochure, make an appointment at the same time. When you get a request for proposal, try to change some of the terms to favor your selection.

2. Speaking before asking. Does a doctor tell you where he went to medical school? No. How many years he's been practicing? No. He asks, "Where does it hurt?" *Flawless:* Ask compelling questions. Ask questions that reveal pain or emotion. Ask questions your competition doesn't ask.

3. Making a verbal agreement for services to be provided. Nothing more fatal than a prospect thinking there is more to the deal than you do. When the prospect says. "I thought you said…" whatever follows is a problem. *Flawless:* Write down and repeat back ALL promises and terms.

4. Negatively referring to the competition. Okay, they're a bunch of dirty rotten creeps. What's your point? When you put them down, you degrade yourself. *Flawless:* Always refer to the competition as "industry standard" and "my worthy competition."

5. Following up to see if you "got my literature," and to see if you "have any questions." The salesman thinks he is being seen as helpful and professional but he's a pest and looks dumb. *Flawless:* Call with ideas and smart questions.

6. Asking "what will it take to get your business?" THE worst question in sales. Will ALWAYS lead to lies, lower price points, and a loss of respect from buyer to salesman. *Flawless:* "I'd like a brief opportunity to share with you why some of my customers bought from me because I'm NOT the lowest price."

7. Assuming the prospect hasn't heard this crap. It's likely that the prospect has a preconceived notion about your company, your product, or both. You may want to change this before you start. *Flawless:* make them ask for a demo or a sales pitch. *Flawless:* Ask "What's been your experience with _____ so far?" or "How would you describe my product to me?"

8. Assuming the prospect hasn't made up his or her mind. Your reputation may have preceded you, your prospect may have already decided to buy from someone else, or your prospect may have already decided to buy from you, and is using your sales presentation to "confirm" rather than "decide." *Flawless:* Make friends as fast as you can before you start. Ask a few questions about where they are on the decision-making scale.

9. Adding nothing of interest or value to the prospect when making a follow up call. Follow up calls are loosely defined as "checking on your money." "Did you make a decision yet?" "Yeah pal, we picked you, but we weren't gonna tell you." Hello! *Flawless:* After the proposal or presentation is the best time to create, shine ,and be memorable. Think of information of value to the prospect, not just questions about how to fill your wallet.

10. Trying to overcome objections with your words rather than customer testimonials. An objection is a statement that says "You haven't sold me yet but I'm interested" Flawless: Use testimonials to overcome objections. This is a complex process, but the most (only) powerful way to put the doubt of the prospect to rest. NOTE: if you are forced to use your words, ask compelling (not sharp-angle, old-world-sales-type) questions rather than make statements.

Free Git⫶Bit...Want to know "the big three" fatal flaws of selling? Go to www.gitomer.com, register if you're a first-time visitor, and enter the words BIG THREE in the GitBit box.

*Are you missing opportunities because
you are too focused on obstacles?*

The bridge between
positive and negative

In business, most people focus on what can't get done, rather than
on what can get done. They handicap themselves mentally by telling
themselves, "I can't get the guy on the phone. No one will return my call.
No one will hire me. I overslept. I forgot. I didn't write it down. No one
told me." And then they go into excuse mode by saying, "I didn't have
enough time." Or pathetically, "I am doing the best I can."

Think about how you'd feel if someone brought you the same
circumstances that you're whining about. Would you want to listen, or
would you want to avoid this person at all costs? That answer is obvious.
But there's a better answer, and it lies in your ability "to be or not to be"
positive. (That is the question.) If you focus on the negative – the results
will likely be negative. If you focus on positive anticipation and positive
outcome – then positive results will follow.

*Here are 7.5 on-the-job things you can do to keep the focus, intensity, drive,
and commitment necessary to change your direction from "Woe is me," to
"Whoa, what a life!":*

1. Stop blaming circumstances for your situation. It's not the rain, or the car,
or the phone, or the product – it's YOU. You have a choice in everything
you do. Choose a better way. Don't blame the path, change the path.
Don't blame the situation, change the situation.

2. Stop blaming other people for your situation. Take responsibility for
yourself and your actions. If you are consistently blaming other people,
guess what, Bubba, get over it – it ain't them.

3. Know your customer or prospect better. Knowing your customer is just
as powerful to prevent problems as it is to handle them. If you can't get
the prospect on the phone, it's your fault for not knowing the best time
to reach him. Know the right time to call. Know when a decision is to be
made. Double confirm every commitment.

4. Persist until you gain an answer. A prospect will respect a tenacious salesperson. If it takes five to ten exposures to make a sale, do you have what it takes to hang in there? Even if it's "No," at least you know where you stand.

5. Know where you are, or where you should be. Manage your time. Have lunch with a customer, not a friend. Keep perfect records. Know enough about your prospect or customer that follow-up becomes easy and fun. Are you organized enough to get to the tenth exposure and have the situation under control enough to make the sale?

6. Work on your skills every day. Books, CDs, seminars. You can never read enough books or listen to enough CDs. I challenge you to do it for an hour a day. One hour a day, seven days a week, for one year, is equal to more than nine full weeks of work. The next time you mindlessly turn on the TV, think about what you could be doing to improve your focus and knowledge base.

7. Become solution oriented. Instead of griping or wallowing in your problems, why not spend the same amount of time working on solutions? Being solution oriented has done more for me and my path to success than any single strategy. Every obstacle presents an opportunity – if you're looking for it. If you're too busy concentrating on the problem, the opportunity will pass you by.

7.5 Think before talking. People speak without thinking, only to regret what they said. Every time you are about to engage someone else, think quickly about what it is you are about to say. How will the words be received? And what else could you be saying that might create a more positive expression? The goal is a positive response or result. The action seems simple, but it requires the most self-discipline. Try it a few times – you'll be amazed at the results.

ATTITUDE OPPORTUNITY: You've been given a bag of cement and a bucket of water. You can either build a stumbling block (a concrete barrier), or a stepping stone (a bridge to wherever you want to go).

The choice is (and always has been) yours. Are you missing opportunities because you are too focused on obstacles?

Don't use a bunch of time-worn
sales ideas to pressure me
to buy when I don't want to.

How the customer wants to be treated, honestly.

To be the best salesperson in the world (and I hope you think you are), you must recognize *listening* as the first commandment of sales. So, I started calling people who buy and asked them what they want salespeople to do. How they want salespeople to act. What they want salespeople to say (or not say). I listened, and I wrote.

Unless you're an order taker, the way you treat (handle) a prospect will determine how often you get the order. And a sale is always made – either you sell the prospect on yes or the prospect sells you on no.

Below is a list of what customers want from salespeople – direct from their mouths. In a nutshell they are saying, "Here's how I want to be sold." How many items on this list can you say you fulfill each time you present your product or service? These customer requests will help you to get yes more often. If you use them in combination, you will have more power to build a relationship and close a sale.

Here's what your customers *have to say about how they want you to act:*

- **JUST GIVE ME THE FACTS.** I don't want a long, drawn-out spiel. After you get to know me a little, get to the point.

- **TELL ME THE TRUTH, AND DON'T USE THE WORD** *HONESTLY*. **IT MAKES ME NERVOUS.** If you say something I doubt or I know not to be true, you're out.

- **I WANT AN ETHICAL SALESPERSON.** Did someone say honest lawyer? Salespeople often get bum raps because of a few without ethics. Your actions will prove your ethics, not your words. (The salespeople who talk ethics usually are without them.)

- **GIVE ME A GOOD REASON WHY THIS PRODUCT/SERVICE IS PERFECT FOR ME.** If I need what you're selling, I need to understand how I benefit from buying it.

- **SHOW ME SOME PROOF.** I'm more likely to buy if you can prove what you say. Show me an article in print reinforcing my confidence, or confirming my decision. (The buyer is saying, "I don't believe most salespeople. They lie just like we do.")

- **SHOW ME I'M NOT ALONE. TELL ME ABOUT A SIMILAR SITUATION WHERE SOMEONE LIKE ME SUCCEEDED.** I don't want to be the first or the only. I need to know how it (or you) has worked elsewhere. I will have a lot more confidence if I know of someone else like me or with the same situation as me who purchased and likes it or did well with it.

- **SHOW ME A LETTER FROM A LOYAL CUSTOMER.** One testimonial has more strength than 100 presentations.

- **TELL ME AND SHOW ME YOU WILL SERVE ME AFTER YOU SELL ME.** I have bought a lot of empty service promises in the past.

- **TELL ME AND SHOW ME THE PRICE IS FAIR.** I want reassurance the price I'm paying is fair for what I'm buying. Make me feel like I'm getting a deal.

- **SHOW ME THE BEST WAY TO PAY.** If I can't afford to pay, but I want what you've got, give me alternatives.

- **GIVE ME A CHOICE AND LET ME DECIDE, BUT MAKE A CONSULTIVE RECOMMENDATION.** Tell me what you would *honestly* (Hey, if I can't say it, neither can you.) do if it was *your* money.

- **REINFORCE MY CHOICE.** I may be nervous I'll make the wrong choice. Help me reinforce my choice with facts that will benefit me and make me feel more confident to buy.

- **DON'T ARGUE WITH ME.** Even if I'm wrong, I don't want some smartass salesperson telling me (or trying to prove) I am. He may win the argument, but he'll lose the sale.

- **DON'T CONFUSE ME.** The more complicated it is, the less likely I am to buy.

- **DON'T TELL ME NEGATIVE THINGS.** I want everything to be great. Don't say bad things about someone else (especially competition), about yourself, about your company, or about me.

- **DON'T TALK DOWN TO ME.** Salespeople think they know everything and think I'm stupid. Don't tell me what *you* think I want to hear. I'm so dumb, I think I'll buy from someone else.

- **DON'T TELL ME WHAT I BOUGHT OR DID IS WRONG.** I want to feel smart and good about what I did. Be tactful if I goofed; show me how others goofed, too.

- **LISTEN TO ME WHEN I TALK.** I'm trying to tell you what I want to buy, and you're too busy trying to sell me what you've got. Shut up and listen.

- **MAKE ME FEEL SPECIAL.** If I'm going to spend my money, I want to feel good about it. It all hinges on your words and actions.

- **MAKE ME LAUGH.** Put me in a good mood and I'm more likely to buy. Making me laugh means I agree with you, and you need my agreement to make a sale.

- **TAKE AN INTEREST IN WHAT I DO.** It may not be important to you, but it's everything to me.

- **BE SINCERE WHEN YOU TELL ME THINGS.** I can tell if you're being phony just to get my money.

- **DON'T USE A BUNCH OF TIME-WORN SALES IDEAS TO PRESSURE ME TO BUY WHEN I DON'T WANT TO.** Don't sound like a salesman. Sound like a friend. Someone trying to help me.

- **DELIVER ME WHAT YOU SELL ME – WHEN YOU SAY YOU WILL**. If I give you my business and you disappoint me, it's unlikely I'll do business with you again.

- **HELP ME BUY – DON'T SELL ME.** I hate being sold, but I love to buy.

I've given you 25 statements made by buyers about how they like to buy. Take another 10 minutes to review how many of the statements you incorporate into your sales presentation and philosophy of selling.

The buyer has the ultimate weapon against your sales idea – he or she can *just say no*. They also have the ultimate weapon for doing it – *their pen*.

Imagine the nerve of your customers and prospects wanting all this stuff. Don't they know you're busy? And why don't they return your phone call anyway?

Return my phone call.

How a salesperson wants to be treated, honestly.

Salespeople have feelings too. If you're a buyer, company owner, or CEO, I ask you – how do you treat salespeople? Would you like to know how they want to be treated?

I have talked to thousands of salespeople who talk about what they wish buyers and prospects would do (or not do). If you're a decision maker for your company, how many of the items below can you *honestly* (there goes that word again) say you do in your relationship with a salesperson?

IMPORTANT NOTE: This section is not about a bunch of whiny salespeople moaning about how they're being mistreated. Rather, it's a series of statements about what salespeople need to build relationships with you, their customers.

If you have ever asked yourself the question, "What do I want as a salesperson?" here are the answers:

- **RETURN MY PHONE CALL.** The number one gripe of salespeople, especially if you got the dreaded *voicemail*. Why can't you take two minutes of your time and return someone's call? Don't you want your call returned?

- **TAKE MY CALL IF YOU'RE IN. IF YOU SCREEN MY CALL, DON'T SCREEN ME OUT.** The other day I called Dick Kittle, president of Associated Mailing, the largest mailing house in the Charlotte area. I said, "Is Dick there?" Next thing I know, a voice says, "Dick Kittle." I said, "Dick, no screen on your calls?" He said, "I don't want to miss any opportunities." And I'll bet he misses darn few.

- **DON'T HAVE YOUR GATEKEEPER SAY, "MR. JOHNSON DOESN'T SEE ANYONE WITHOUT AN APPOINTMENT."** At least have the courtesy of telling Mr. Johnson I'm here and giving him the choice. Jerk.

- **TELL ME THE TRUTH.** I'd rather know the truth than have you string me along, or lie about the situation. Have the guts to be truthful. You want it from me, don't you?

- **IF YOU DON'T DECIDE (OR AREN'T THE ONLY DECISION MAKER), TELL ME, AND TELL ME WHO (OR WHO ELSE) DOES.** Don't waste my time or yours. I like you, but I want to talk to (all) the decision makers.

- **TELL ME HOW YOU FEEL WHILE I'M PRESENTING.** If I'm doing something right or wrong, I want to know so I can help serve you better.

- **GIVE ME YOUR UNDIVIDED ATTENTION DURING MY PRESENTATION.** No phone calls, people running in and out or reading your mail. Thanks.

- **TELL ME YOUR REAL OBJECTION.** If you do, it will help us both. Your true objection will shorten the sales cycle and make us both more productive. You won't hurt my feelings – I really want to know the truth.

- **DO WHAT YOU SAY YOU WILL DO.** *Example*: If you tell me a decision will be made by Wednesday, take my call on the appointed day and tell me the answer. *Example*: You tell me to call you on Friday to set up a meeting. I call. Your secretary says, "Oh, he's out of town and won't be back until Tuesday." Common courtesy. Do what you say. That's not too much to ask. Is it?

- **DON'T TELL ME YOU WANT TO THINK ABOUT IT.** I hate that. Tell me the real objection or how you really feel. Admit it – you've already decided.

- **DON'T TELL ME IT'S NOT IN THE BUDGET OR YOU SPENT YOUR BUDGET FOR THE YEAR.** Tell me how you feel about my product or service and if you want to buy it now, next year, or never.

- **IF YOU DON'T HAVE THE MONEY AND YOU WANT TO BUY, TELL ME, SO I CAN HELP YOU FIND A WAY TO BUY.** Don't let pride or ego get in the way of the selling process. Salespeople run into people without money all the time (too much of the time, actually) – but still want to help.

- **DON'T PLAY GAMES.** Don't say, "I can get it for $500 less. Will you match the price?" or "I'm going to shop around to see if your deal is the best, then I might call you back." Be straight up with me. Put your cards on the table if you want a long-term relationship (like I do).

- **RESPECT ME.** Often common courtesy will do more to enhance our relationship than anything (besides a big order).

- **IF YOU MUST MEET WITH OTHERS TO GET A FINAL DECISION, LET ME BE THERE TOO.** So I can answer questions about my product or service that are sure to arise.

- **BE ON TIME FOR OUR APPOINTMENT.** I don't want to wait. It's not fair to appoint me at 10 and take me at 10:30 and say, "I'm sorry. I got tied up." I'll say, "That's OK," but it ain't what I'm thinking. Be as timely as you would want me to be.
- **SHOW UP FOR YOUR APPOINTMENT.** Sometimes you say, "Oh, it's just a salesman. What's the difference?" The difference is common courtesy. Show me you're as dependable as you want me to be.
- **DECIDE NOW.** You already know the answer. Why don't you just tell me?
- **GIVE ME THE SALE WHEN I ASK FOR IT.** Even though this is a fantasy request, I couldn't resist putting it in a list of things salespeople want.

And hey, Mr. CEO – who had no time for, is rude to, and won't return the calls of salespeople – I ask you this: *Do you have salespeople? Are you treating salespeople the same way you want your salespeople treated in a selling situation?* Think about it next time you don't return a phone call from a salesperson.

It's amazing to me how simple the sales process would be if buyers just followed one rule. *The Golden Rule.*

Maybe if it was revised for sales and given to CEOs and decision makers, it would have an impact. *Here it is for the first time...*

The Golden Rule of Sales for CEOs
Do unto salespeople as you would have buyers and decision makers do unto *your* salespeople.

*The hot button is a bridge that can get you
from the presentation to the sale.*

The elusive hot button.
How do you find it?

All sales training includes this line: *If you want to make the sale, be sure
to push a hot button.* Great, where's that? It's within plain sight; it's within
asking distance; it's within listening distance.

All you have to do is be alert.

*Pushing the hot button only works if you can find it. Here are some ways
to discover or uncover a personal or business hot button in a conversation
(NOTE WELL: personal is hotter than business):*

- **ASK QUESTIONS ABOUT STATUS AND SITUATION –** Where he
  vacationed. Where his kid goes to college. Where the business
  stands at the moment. Where it came from (history).

- **ASK QUESTIONS ABOUT ISSUES OF PRIDE –** Biggest success in
  business. Biggest goal this year.

- **ASK QUESTIONS ABOUT PERSONAL INTERESTS –** What he does with
  most of his free time. What sports or hobbies he pursues.

- **ASK WHAT HE WOULD DO IF HE DIDN'T HAVE TO WORK –** What his
  real dreams and ambitions are.

- **ASK GOAL-RELATED QUESTIONS –** What is the prime objective of
  his company this year? How is he going to meet that objective?
  What does he see as his biggest barrier to the goal?

- **LOOK AT EVERYTHING IN THE OFFICE –** Look for something
  outstanding. Something framed apart from others, or looking
  bigger, more prominent. Look for pictures and awards. Ask how
  he got them.

Asking and looking are the easy parts. Listening is the hard part. Listening is the important part. *The hot button is in the answer!*

1. Listen to the first thing said or alluded to. What is first said in response to a question is what is foremost in the mind of the respondent. The thing most on your mind is usually what you talk about first. It may not be the actual hot button – but it will provide insights to it.

2. Listen for the tone of first responses. The tone will depict the urgency or importance. His gestures and loudness will indicate passion.

3. Listen for immediate, emphatic responses. Knee-jerk reactions are hot subjects. Absolute agreement.

4. Listen for a long, drawn-out explanation or story. Something told in detail is usually compelling (and hot).

5. Listen to repeated statements. Something said twice is at the front of the mind.

5.5 Look for emotional responses. Something said with passion or in a different tone.

OK, you think you found it. Now, let's push it.

Here are 4.5 button-pushing ideas:

1. Ask questions about importance or significance. Questions that will help you understand the situation better. *What's the importance of that to you? How will that impact you?*

2. Ask questions about the area you think is hot. If you have taken notes, there are some areas to probe that will generate heat.

3. Ask questions in a subtle way. Work them into the pitch as a part of the conversation, and watch the reaction. If you believe it's a *hot button*, offer solutions that satisfy that circumstance.

4. Don't be afraid to bring up the hot button throughout the presentation. Reconfirm it and listen for emphasis of response from the prospect.

4.5 Use "If I (offer a solution), would you (commit or buy)?" and variations. Try "There's a way…" This type of question or statement gets a true response because it consists of a possible solution that hits the button.

Words of caution:

- **THE *HOT BUTTON* IS SOMETIMES A VERY SENSITIVE ISSUE.** It may have other ramifications that the prospect is not willing to divulge. Your job is to uncover the button and use it to make the sale. Use your best judgment. If you sense the issue is touchy, don't push too hard.

- **THE *HOT BUTTON* IS ELUSIVE.** But you can find it with a question or observation. The hot button is a prize you can win if you listen to the prospect with care. The hot button is a bridge that can get you from the presentation to the sale.

- **THE *HOT BUTTON* IS AN ELEVATOR.** It will go all the way to the top floor (the sale). But it only works if you push the button.

The hot button is a bridge that can get you from the presentation to the sale. All you gotta do is find it. How do you find it? "Elementary, my dear Watson." In 1888, Sherlock Holmes said, "It is a capital offense to theorize before one has data." You gotta be a detective to find the hot button.

*"May I offer a bit of constructive criticism?
When you're having lunch with a client, don't
carve little dollar signs in your mashed potatoes."*

"Listening is the hard part. Listening is the important part. The hot button is in the prospect's response."

— Jeffrey Gitomer

THE SALES BIBLE

Part 1
The Rules. The Secrets. The Fun.

The Book of BIG Secrets

1.4

Eh, Confidentially, Doc

Big Secrets…

Okay, okay. We've established the fact that I can't keep a secret.

I knew that! But neither can you, loose lips.

Here are some deep, dark ones. A treasure map that will lead you to El Dorado.

Well, not actually, but if you follow these secrets, you can buy an El Dorado.

*Your best competitor couldn't blast
you away from a customer
who is also a friend.*

More sales are made with friendship than salesmanship.

Your mom said it best. As a child, when you were fighting or arguing with a sibling or friend, your mom would say, "Billy, you know better than that! Now you make friends with Johnny."

Your mother never told you to use the alternative-of-choice close or the sharp-angle close on Johnny. She never said to quote Johnny with our policy. She just said make friends.

That may have been one of the most powerful sales and service lessons you ever got.

There's an old business adage that says, "All things being equal, people want to do business with their friends. And all things being NOT so equal, people STILL want to do business with their friends." It is estimated that 50% of sales are made because of friendship. I say the number is higher.

In the South, it's called "the good old boy network." In the North, they say it's "who you know," but it's really just friendship selling.

If you think you're going to get the sale because you have the best product, the best service, or the best price – *dream on, Bubba*. You're not even half right. If 50% of sales are made on a friendly basis, and you haven't made friends with the prospect (or customer), you're missing 50% of your market.

Friends don't need to sell friends using sales techniques. Think about it. You don't need sales techniques when you ask a friend out, or ask for a favor – you just ask. Wanna make more sales? **YOU DON'T NEED MORE SALES TECHNIQUES; YOU NEED MORE FRIENDS.**

Think about your best customers. How did they get that way? Don't you have great relationships with them? If you're friends with your best customers, it will often eliminate the need for price checking, price negotiating, and delivery time demands. You can even *occasionally* screw up and still keep them.

There's another huge bonus to being friends – competition is virtually eliminated. Your fiercest competitor couldn't blast you away from a customer who is also a friend.

Most salespeople think that unless they are calling a customer to sell something that it's a wasted call. Nothing could be further from the truth. ***People don't like to be sold, but they love to buy.***

How do you start building friendship and relationships? Slowly. It takes time to develop a relationship. It takes time to build a friendship. If you're reading this and thinking "I don't have time for this relationship stuff, I'm too busy making sales," find a new profession – this one won't last long.

A different venue than the office will begin building friendships and relationships. Here are a few places to meet or take your customer:

- **A ball game.**
- **The theater.**
- **A concert.**
- **A gallery crawl.**
- **A chamber of commerce after-hours event.**
- **A community help project.**
- **A breakfast, a lunch, a dinner.**
- **A seminar given by your company.**
- **If your customer has kids, get a few tickets to an I-Max theater. Go on the weekend. Talk about solidifying a relationship. An I-Max movie is great fun, and it ain't just for kids.**

BIG MISTAKE: If you have tickets to an event, don't just give the tickets to your customer. GO WITH the customer. You can learn a lot (and give value to a relationship) spending a few quality hours with the people who provide money to your company.

Join a business association and get involved. I belong to the Metrolina Business Council. MBC is a 27-year-old group of business owners and managers whose main objective is to do business with one another and help members get business. But MBC is not just about business, it's about relationships and friendships – ask any member.

CAUTION: This does not eliminate your need to be a master salesman. You must know sales ideas to capture the other half of the market. So keep reading books and listening to those CDs in your car.

Moving from the North (Cherry Hill, New Jersey) to the South (Charlotte, North Carolina) helped me understand the value of business friends. They're much easier to establish in the South. And they tend to be more loyal.

I'm often in conversations where someone is lamenting the fact they can't get into or around the so-called "good old boy" network. That is the biggest bunch of baloney, and lamest sales excuse I've heard. All the salesperson is saying is that he has failed to bring anything of value to the table and failed to establish a relationship or make a friend – *and someone else has.*

You can only earn a commission using a sales idea, but you can earn a fortune building friendships and relationships.

If you make a sale,
you earn a commission.

If you make a friend,
you can earn a fortune.

Free Git✗Bit... **Want a few words of caution about the elusive hot button?** Go to www.gitomer.com, register if you're a first-time visitor, and enter the words HOT BUTTON in the GitBit box.

Your present customer has a history of buying,
has credit terms, likes your product, and likes you…
What are you waiting for?

Your best new prospects are your present customers.

Looking for new prospects? Who isn't! It may interest you to know that you have hundreds of HOT prospects you're not paying attention to. They're your present customers.

Consider these 10.5 assets already in your favor:

1. They know you.
2. They like you.
3. You have established rapport.
4. Confidence and trust have been built.
5. You have a history of delivery.
6. They respect you.
7. They use (and like) your product or service.
8. They will return your call.
9. They will be more receptive to your presentation and product offering.
10. They have credit and have paid you in the past.
10.5 They don't have to be sold – they will buy.

THINK ABOUT THIS: You're a farmer. You decide to milk your neighbor's cows, instead of your own. You walk by your barn, your cows are full of milk – udders so full they're begging for a set of hands – but you pass them by and head for your neighbors in search of milk.

HERE'S A CLUE: It's the same in sales. Why would you go out and cold call a prospect when your present customer base is ready to be milked? They're waiting for you. Dripping with business. I don't think you could ask for much more than that. It beats a cold call by 1,000 to 1.

Here are some ideas to get your present customers to buy more – now:

Sell them something new. People love to buy new things. Your enthusiasm will set the tone. Create excitement about how your new (better) product will be exactly what will serve better or produce more. Sell sizzle. Sell appointments. Then let them buy.

Sell them an upgrade or an enhancement. Bigger, better, faster. Enhancements and upgrades have kept the computer software industry profitable since its inception. Upselling has built fortunes – just ask any fast food business. (The question, "Do you want fries with that?" sells billions of fries annually.)

Sell them more of the same in a different place. Look for other uses, other departments, growth or expansion of the customer's company, or replacement due to wear and tear. You may have to dig a little, but the soil is softer at a present customer's place of business than the pile of rocks you usually face at a new prospect's company.

Sell them additional products and services. Your company may sell multiple products or offer varied services, and very few of your customers carry your full line. Sometimes a customer will say, "Oh, I didn't know you sold that." When you hear a customer say that, DON'T BLAME THE SALESPERSON – blame the salesperson's trainer.

Get your customers to meet you for lunch. If you can get the customer out of their office environment, you can often uncover more opportunities for them to buy. Ask them to bring a referral along. Bring a referral for them. Build the relationship, and you'll build more sales.

Get them to give you one referral a month. This is the true report card on the job your product or service has done in performing for your customers, as well as a report card on your ability to gain enough buyer confidence that they will refer you to a friend or business associate.

Give them one referral a month. Getting your customer business will create new thought patterns in the way they perceive you. If you get them business, they will find new ways and new people to do the same for you.

NOTE: No matter whether you make a sale or not, continuing to be in front of your customer builds relationship and goodwill.

If you can't call on your present customers, or if you come up with some lame excuse like, "I've sold them everything I can sell them," what it really means is:

1. **You have failed to establish enough rapport with the customer.**

2. **You have probably not followed up well (or at all) after the sale.**

3. **Your customer has some problem and you're reluctant to call and open a can of worms.**

4. **You're in need of more sales and creativity training.**

4.5 **You have not developed a proper relationship with the customer.**

Most salespeople think that unless they are calling a customer to sell something, it's a wasted call. Nothing could be farther from the truth.

I'm amazed at the salespeople who make a sale and move on to the next prospect.

I challenge you to carefully (and honestly) look at your customer list. I'll bet there are hundreds of opportunities to sell something.

I would rather have 100 loyal customers to do business with than 1,000 prospects.

The secret to a great week is to use Monday as a springboard. Schedule your hottest prospect for Monday morning.

Make a sale on Monday.
It does wonders for your week.

I'm often asked if there is some secret for consistent sales performance. The answer is simple: *Have a great Monday* and *Have a great Friday*.

How you do on the first day of the week sets the tone for the rest of it. And how you do on Monday is based entirely on how smart you worked last week. If you're disciplined enough to follow these methods, you won't believe the difference it will make in your week, and your productivity.

If you're looking for consistency in selling performance, try these 8.5 steps:

1. Make a sale first thing Monday morning. Set an appointment for early Monday morning that you're confident will buy. It will make you feel great to capture a sale to start your week. It will set you in motion and give you a mental boost to work harder (and make another one).

NOTE WELL: Since there are a lot of companies having sales meetings on Monday morning, be as productive as you can be with an appointment. Start making calls immediately after your meeting. And, if time permits, make calls in the early morning. Lots of decision makers are early risers.

2. Learn something new. Pop a training or motivational CD into your car or home stereo (or both), and instead of listening to the same old news or music, try to feed your head with new knowledge that will help you make that first sale. When you learn a new idea on the way to an appointment, you can try it out in minutes.

3. Make at least five appointments for the rest of the week. Why not have a Monday full of success and positive anticipation? It's up to you. Pick up the phone and work at it.

4. Work like hell all week – especially on Friday. How you do on the last day sets the tone for the next week. Most people slack off. If you work intensely on Friday, it will ensure success next week and give you a good reason to have a great weekend.

5. Learn something new. Continuing your sales education throughout the week on a regularly scheduled basis is as important to your success as any other aspect of sales. But make sure you listen on Friday morning.

6. Make a sale on Friday afternoon. Schedule a close for Friday afternoon. There's nothing like ending the week on a positive note.

7. Confirm and solidify your Monday appointment on Friday. If you worked hard the last four days, you've already set your Monday morning make-a-sale appointment. Call the prospect on Friday and confirm it.

8. Make at least five appointments for next week. Why not guarantee yourself a full schedule next week? Spend your weekend relaxing instead of worrying about how few appointments you have. Make this commitment to yourself: I won't leave work on Friday until I have five appointments and I've set my Monday appointment/sale.

8.5 The secret to a great week is to use Monday as a springboard. The big secret is to trigger it by making a sales call on Monday morning. The bigger secret is having enough qualified prospects in your pipeline to make your Monday sale possible. BIGGEST SECRET: Keep your pipeline full.

It sounds simple.

Make appointments, listen to CDs, make sales. It is simple; it just isn't easy. But if you work intensely, you can do it.

I CAN MAKE ONE PROMISE TO YOU. Follow these guidelines and you'll have sales consistency and money. Now you know the secret. I've give you the answer. The question is *what will you DO with the answer?*

Free GitBit...**Want to know what the Guggenheim Museum in New York City has in common with sales success?** Go to www.gitomer.com, register if you're a first-time visitor, and enter the words TOP DOWN SELLING in the GitBit box.

I urge you to write yours. It builds your
character at the same time it lays it bare.

Your personal mission statement.

A personal mission statement is your affirmation, philosophy, and purpose rolled into one. It's an opportunity to bring your goals into focus and transfer your ideals into the real world.

It's a chance for you to write your own legacy. It's your personal challenge to yourself. Sounds pretty heavy, but actually it's fun if you do it right.

Here are the ground rules:
- **Define yourself.**
- **Define what you're dedicated to.**
- **Define your service to others.**
- **Define how you will strive to get better, do new things, and grow.**
- **Define your commitment to yourself.**
- **Define your commitment to others.**
- **Define how you're going to achieve your mission.**

Here are words that will help... will, dedication, persist, honest, ethical, positive, enthusiastic, fun, health, learn new things, listen, help, provide, encourage, others, continually, example.

Use your goals and visions to define your mission:
- **The examples you seek to set.**
- **The ideals by which you live or seek to live.**
- **The affirmations that you can use every day to become a better person.**

THE PROCESS TAKES TIME. Write a first draft. Let it sit for a few days. Re-read it slowly and make changes that you feel better express your true feelings. Describe the things you think you are and the things you seek to accomplish or become.

Don't be afraid or embarrassed to flatter yourself. You're writing this for yourself, not others. Affirm everything you think you are or think you want to become. Do it with a sense of pride and a spirit of adventure.

Post it where you can see it every day. Sign it in big, bold felt-tip pen.

Live it. Live it every day.

I'm attaching mine to use as a template for yours. Feel free to paraphrase. I'm sharing mine because it has helped me achieve some tough goals in some tough times.

I urge you to write yours. It builds your character at the same time it lays it bare. It serves as a beacon of light in the fog of life. It is a path to take that you build on every day. It is your mission.

"My old mission statement was more eloquent, and dignified, but not nearly as effective."

Jeffrey Gitomer
Personal Mission Statement

I am a father...
I will be a positive person and positive example.
I will encourage my children, give them self-confidence,
and help them understand the ways of the world.

I will be a good person...
I will help others when I am able, without sacrificing my goals.
I will say yes when I can, no when I can't.
I will be the type of friend to others that they hope I'll be.
I will not be ashamed or embarrassed to ask for help when I need it.

I will seek business leadership positions...
I will continue to be a leader by example
in my writings about sales, customer service, and personal development.

My expertise and technology will position me to serve...
businesses and individuals with the highest-quality plans, reports,
training, advice, business expertise, and customer support.

I will strive to build quality, long-term relationships...
with my customers and vendors, and to deal fairly and honestly
with all people and companies I encounter. I will continually
endeavor to increase the level of service to my customers.

I will help my customers discover the best solutions...
to their sales, customer service, and personal development needs by
listening, providing information, and performing services to the highest
standard of excellence.

I will serve my community...
in ways that reflect my commitment to co-workers,
customers, and friends;
and show my appreciation for the help and support they and
the community have given me.

**I will be the best person I can be for myself so I can be my best
when helping others. I will be enthusiastic in all that I do.
I will do my best to maintain my health.
I will try to learn something new every day.
I will have fun every day.
I will rededicate myself to my positive attitude every day.**

THE SALES BIBLE

Part 1
The Rules. The Secrets. The Fun.

The Book of Humor

Laugh Last!

Humor...

If you're serious about succeeding at a sales career, it's time you started looking on the lighter side.

Go ahead, make me laugh.

Humor melts ice.
It warms the coldest of hearts.
It makes sales.

They'll be laughing all the way to the bank...
your bank.

1.5

If I can get the prospect or customer to laugh,
I can get him or her to buy…So can you.

A funny thing happened to me on the way to a sale!

When you're on sales calls and prospects tell you no, start thanking them. Tell them that by saying *no*, they're helping you get one step closer to *yes*. Tell them how much you appreciate it. Tell them it takes you five no's to get one yes and you still need three more no's. *Ask them if they know anyone else who might not be interested, so that you can get the three more no's before someone says yes.* Tell them you need people to tell you *no*, because it helps you get to yes quicker. It'll blow them away. Humor. How much of it do you employ when selling? Enough to make a sale?

HUMOR IS ONE OF THE MOST IMPORTANT COMMUNICATION STRENGTHS TO MASTER IN THE SELLING PROCESS. If you can get the prospect or customer to laugh, you can get him or her to buy.

NOTHING BUILDS RAPPORT FASTER THAN HUMOR. It's a bonding mechanism that transcends (and reveals) all prejudice and prejudgments. It brings the selling process to a real level. It brings out the truth. I have found that many truths are revealed through humor. If you listen carefully to a prospect's jokes, it will often reveal philosophy, prejudice, and intelligence (or lack of it).

Here are a few guidelines for how you can use humor to make more sales:

- **Use humor in the warm-up of the presentation to set a happy tone for the meeting.** The earlier you get a prospect to laugh, the better. Laughter is a form of approval.

- **Don't make jokes at someone else's expense.** If the prospect knows the person (you never know who knows who), or is related to the person at the brunt end of the joke, you're dead meat. If it is repeated, I guarantee it will be mistold or altered, and will surely come back to haunt you.

- **Use yourself as the example or victim of the joke.** It shows you're human and can take it. It's also a safe form of humor.

- **Some people won't get the joke.** Silence at the end of a joke is pretty horrifying. Make sure it's funny to someone else before you tell it where it counts. But no matter how tested the material, some people's elevator stops before the top floor, and they will never get it.

- **Don't use ethnic humor or make ethnic jokes unless you're the ethnic.** That's not a guideline, that's a rule. I was challenged by a friend who said that telling someone an ethnic joke is implied approval for others to tell one. I have mixed feelings about that. I go back to truth in humor, and I'd rather have the prospect reveal himself or herself. But I do respect my friend's opinion.

- **Listen before you tell a joke.** Try to determine the type and demeanor of the person or people you're addressing. The wrong humor will kill you as fast as the right humor will let you live (and sell) eternally.

- **Use personal experience rather than retold jokes.** Talk about something funny that happened in your office, or with your kid, or when you were a kid rather than "two guys were walking down the street..."

- **If you tell a joke that prospects or customers have heard before, it is actually a negative to make them hear it again.** That's one great reason for using personal humor – they are sure to be hearing it for the first time.

- **Timing. Timing. Timing.** Humor properly inserted will turn the prospect or crowd in your favor. But be forewarned – there is *never* a right time for a political or religious joke told to someone you don't know. Don't use humor where it's not appropriate.

- **Keep a joke file.** Write down funny things or events so that you can remember them in selling or speaking situations.

- **There are humor tendencies.** Men and women tend to make jokes about the other gender. Religious groups are apt to take each other on. People in bordering states tend to be on the wrong end of the joke. In North Carolina, it seems to be about farmers in West Virginia. But when I lived in Indiana, it was those farmers from Kentucky. And of course if you're from New York, everyone else in the world is a farmer.

- **Risqué jokes can be risky.** They will get you in trouble if you say them to the wrong person. Know the limits of your audience before engaging your mouth.

- **Turn questions into opportunities with humor.** You give a 30-second phone pitch and ask for an appointment at the end. *The prospect asks,* "How much does this cost?" *You say,* "Oh, I don't charge to make a sales call."

- **Don't dread cold calls; laugh them off.** There is a fear and dislike many salespeople have when it comes to cold calling. A salesman told me a story that he had a big fear of being thrown out of a company when making a cold call. I suggested to him that his strategy should be to only cold call on one-story buildings.

- **Adapt real-world humor to a real-world selling situation.** I was making a presentation in a room full of smokers. I hate smoke. So I recounted a story where I was driving with my friend, Becky Brown, and she was talking about how tough it was to quit smoking and how hard she was trying but just couldn't. I asked, "Have you ever tried the gum – you know, that nicotine gum?" She said, "I tried it, but I couldn't keep it lit." I made the sale. If you can make 'em laugh, you can make 'em buy.

"The roof leaks, the furnace doesn't work, and the plumbing needs repair but it's located on the greatest planet in the universe!"

The Bookof WOW!

> "I am the greatest!"
> — *Muhammed Ali*

Are you just another (business) card-carrying salesperson?

Does your pitch come straight out of a (tin) can?

Are they going to forget you as soon as you walk out of the door?

Are they going to take your calls again? Return them?

If you're not outstanding in front of the prospect, you'll be out standing in the street.

The WOW! factor separates you from others.
Using WOW! turns your prospect into a customer.

The WOW! factor.
Use it to land the big sale.

WOW! is your ability to be different. The WOW! factor and your closing ratio have lots in common. If you don't WOW! 'em, it's likely you won't sell 'em. I went to New York to sell a publisher on a book idea based on my successful column on selling skills, Sales Moves. I used the WOW! factor.

BACKGROUND AND PREPARATION. I developed a total WOW! preparation. I had sample prototype book cover designs and mock-ups; I had a 15-page proposal including several letters of reference; I named the book *The Sales Bible*; I had the name trademarked; I had a multimedia presentation prepared; I had a daring marketing concept incorporating a computer disk and a package of wallet-sized flashcards to make it different from all other books on the shelf; I wrote my pitch and answers to every objection I could think of; I selected clothing I thought was appropriate; I was ready.

I selected ten target publishers and contacted four before I arrived in New York. I made one solid appointment with the publisher I really wanted (a major publishing firm) with a guy I'll call Mr. Book.

THIS IS HOW THE APPOINTMENT WAS MADE. It took me seven calls to get Mr. Book's name and extension number! Call number eight – BINGO. He answers his own phone. (He later said, "The phone is usually more important than what I'm doing.") I tell Mr. Book everything he needs to know in about 1.5 minutes – he seems interested. I tell him I'll send him a proposal and I ask him for a five-minute appointment. He says, "The old five-minute appointment bit. Did you read that in the Harvey Mackay book?"

I said, "Listen, Harvey Mackay is from Minnesota. I'm from Jersey. He learned that ploy from me!" Mr. Book laughed and said okay to a five-minute appointment. (I sent Mr. Book my package by next-day air.)

I HAD TWO MENTORS HELP ME WITH MY PRESENTATION. Ty Boyd, the voice of Charlotte for two decades and one of the nicest people I've ever met, who put me on the right path; and Bill Lewis, who was in Manhattan and had published 20 books. (Every day I showed up at his place for an hour of coaching and encouragement. He was instrumental to my success.)

THE FIRST APPOINTMENT. I walk into Mr. Book's office in midtown Manhattan and he says, "Okay, Gitomer. I've read your proposal. You've got five minutes." I start in immediately with background, get to the meat of my presentation in less than two minutes, put my prototype in his hands, sneak in two personal questions (for rapport), and finish my pitch in less than five minutes. Then I begin to question, listen, and take notes. (The longer he talks, the more questions he asks, the stronger my chances are.) *Forty-five minutes later, I'm still in there.*

Mr. Book says, "I'm interested. Leave your stuff and let me run it by my CEO." Great, I thought. These were the only copied I had.

But wait. I've got three other publishers to see in the next three days, and this guy wants to keep half my tools.

"When will you be meeting?" I ask lightly. "Before the end of the week," he says, trying to gain a position of power. (Here goes my risk statement.)

"I have a slight dilemma, and I need your help," I said. "I've got several appointments over the next few days. Do you think you might have a chance to discuss this with the CEO by tomorrow?"

"I should be able to," he said.

"Great. Why don't we set up an appointment for the end of the day tomorrow?" I said, nailing him to the floor. "4:30 okay?" I ask. He said, "Looks fine to me."

I'm so excited I could scream. I walk back to my hotel singing and dancing. (In Manhattan you can do anything you want. No one notices, looks, or cares.)

I get back to my room and there's a phone message from Mr. Book under my door. I call. He says, "Can you make it a little earlier? I want to have a few other people present."

"Yeah, sure," I reply in a millisecond. (If you ever want a dictionary definition of a buying signal, that was it.)

THE SECOND APPOINTMENT. I arrive ten minutes early the next day. Mr. Book leads me into a conference room so that I can hook up my computerized presentation. In walks the national sales manager. I have to convince him why my book will sell. I turn on my computerized multi-media dog-and-pony show that has him leaning so far forward he about falls out of the chair. Now it's time to drag out every tool in my box. I talk about additional distribution ideas I have. I tell him I would be glad to go with him on selected sales calls. He is now totally convinced he can sell it.

We then negotiate "What if we accept you" terms. Advances. Royalties. Publicity. Mr. Book asks, "If I offer you this deal (he lists the bullet points) will you take it?" (There's a switch. Now *he's* closing me!) "Yes," I say. "I'll call you by noon tomorrow and let you know," he says and walks out of the room.

Eighteen more hours of agony...

THE THIRD APPOINTMENT. By 1:00PM, no call. I call him. He gruffly says he hasn't met Mr. Big yet and will call later. Tactically I tell him I'll stop by at the end of the day to pick up some of my materials. He says okay. I'm a nervous wreck. At 3:30, he leaves a message for me. I decide not to call back. At 4:45, I show up at his office. He keeps me waiting until 5:20. He comes out to greet me and says the magic words, Let's talk business.

WOW! I just made the biggest sale of my life!

NOTE: In success, there are always failures. In all, I contacted ten publishers and two agents. All were cold calls. Six publishers turned me down or I said I needed an agent to talk with them. One agent said no; the other has yet to call me back.

I'm saving the rejection letters so I can frame them around my book.

I really don't know if I would have made the sale having pulled out all the WOW! stops at the other publishers. WOW! doesn't work all the time. But it works more than non-WOW!

WOW! takes courage to use and skill to execute. I was prepared to use mine, and fortunate enough to succeed. I recommend that you prepare to use WOW! so that you can increase your chances to win with it.

The WOW! factor can be used by anyone.
The problem is that most salespeople
won't sacrifice enough to create it.

Are you using the WOW! factor?

One of the most powerful aspects of sales is being different.

What is WOW!? WOW! is sales.
WOW! separates the strong from the weak.
WOW! separates the sincere from the insincere.
WOW! separates the sales pros from the cons.
WOW! separates YES from NO.
WOW! is the full measure of your sales power and the way you use it.

Are you WOW!? Is WOW! a factor in your selling process?
How do you WOW! the customer?

You can measure how much WOW! is in your sales effort by evaluating
yourself against the following 8.5 guidelines of how to be WOW!:

1. Be persistent. To reach the prospect, to get the prospect your information, to get information about the prospect, to appoint the prospect.

2. Be knowledgeable about the prospect. Your knowledge of the prospect and his or her business is often critical to completing the sale. Use the famous "Mackay 66" questionnaire as a guideline for how much information is needed. Go to www.gitomer.com, register if you are a first-time visitor, and enter the word MACKAY66 in the GitBit box.

3. Be prepared. Have a perfect presentation that you've rehearsed. Have a written proposal for what you want to accomplish or sell. Develop support tools and support documentation. Identify all possible objections, and prescript, test, and rehearse responses for each of them.

4. Be ten minutes early. It's best to arrive a little early. It's always a disaster to arrive late. Carry a light load (only what you need for the show).

5. Be professional. Great clothing, professional accessories; briefcase, business cards. Have everything crisp and clean.

6. Get to the point quickly. Then question, listen, and question. Talk straight to the point. Get your meat out in five minutes or less. Write down your thoughts when the prospect is talking. Don't interrupt.

7. Separate yourself from your competition and everyone else. Have creative, new ideas. Have the sale in finished form (design done, preliminary layout, sample). Have a WOW! presentation. Have a comparison chart of key areas where you beat the competition. Do things no one else would do.

8. Be confident in what you say and the way you act. Build rapport first and keep building it during the presentation. Use humor, use humor, use humor. Act and speak as though the deal were done. Use your manners. Think back to your mother screaming at you about how to act civilized and do it. Don't confuse confidence with cockiness. One works; the other fails.

8.5 Be WOW! yourself. You must be positive, enthusiastic, focused, polished, and convinced. You must be outstanding enough to be memorable.

Here are 15 characteristics/words that epitomize a WOW! salesperson:

WOW! Factor	My score: 1=lowest, 5=highest
1. Persistent (relentless)	1 2 3 4 5
2. Prepared	1 2 3 4 5
3. Best	1 2 3 4 5
4. Creatively different	1 2 3 4 5
5. Funny	1 2 3 4 5
6. Truthful	1 2 3 4 5
7. Real (genuine)	1 2 3 4 5
8. Compelling	1 2 3 4 5
9. Fast and to the point	1 2 3 4 5
10. Skillful	1 2 3 4 5
11. Knowledgeable	1 2 3 4 5
12. Courageous	1 2 3 4 5
13. Memorable	1 2 3 4 5
14. Long term	1 2 3 4 5
15. Able to get to *yes*	1 2 3 4 5

Add up your score and rate yourself.

$$70\text{-}75 = \text{WOW!}$$
$$60\text{-}69 = \text{AOK}$$
$$50\text{-}59 = \text{SO?}$$
$$15\text{-}49 = \text{DUD}$$

Getting to WOW! is identifying your weaknesses in the preceding 15 areas, making a plan to strengthen them one by one, developing the self-discipline to carry out your plan, and taking action to practice and implement the changes. You can do it – if you want it bad enough.

Are you WOW!? Ask yourself:

- **Would I buy it if I were the buyer?**

- **Do I have what it takes to stick with it, stick to it, and do it until it's done?**

- **Will the prospect be moved to act as a result of my presentation?**

- **Will the prospect go home or around the office and talk about me in a positive way?**

- **Do I epitomize the 15 WOW! characteristics?**

There is a challenge and sacrifice needed to put WOW! into your selling process. If you have the fortitude to put the package together, then you must put your WOW! in front of the prospect.

Here are the final steps to incorporate WOW! into your presentation. Notice that all are intangible:

- **Focus on your target.**

- **Have your dreams ever present in your mind.**

- **Put your passion in your presentation.**

- **Don't ever let them see you sweat.**

- **Let them feel your belief in yourself and your product.**

- **Never quit.**

In sales, it all boils down to one word. YES! To get there more often, use WOW!

When you leave an appointment or a
networking event, will anyone remember
that you were there?

Remember me? I'm a salesman. Just like all the others.

My cat Lito had a business card. She was our *Corporate Mascot* and played a vital role in my office productivity. Whenever I needed an important paper, Lito was lying on it. I gave her card out in seminars and training programs for fun and a laugh. And everyone who got her card kept it, showed it to someone else, talked about it, and talked to me.

> Being memorable is creating a vivid image in the mind of the prospect that distinguishes you from others. What you do. How you do it. What you say. How you say it.

How memorable are you? Do your prospects talk about you when you're gone? Or are they talking about (and ordering from) your competitor?

Here are some recommendations and examples of things I've seen that are memorable – and brought about business:

Spend money on your business cards. They are the image you project about the quality of your business. Take a look at your business card. Will customers and prospects remember you from it? If someone gave it to you, would you make a comment about it?

What makes your business card unique? Do you have a creative title? If your company won't let you have a non-traditional title on your card, make your own!

HERE'S THE CLUE: Business cards are not an expense. They're your image! They're not a marker. Theyr're your marketing piece. Make them so cool that someone is compelled to show someone else.

Get with the times. Want your business cards to be current with the rest of the business world? Better pull yours out of your wallet and double check that you've got the basics covered. *Does your business card (and every one of your employees' business cards) have the following information?*

- **Name**
- **Title**
- **Company name**
- **Company address**
- **E-mail address**

- **Company's Web site address**
- **Phone (with area code)**
- **Fax (with area code)**
- **Cell phone (with area code)**
- **Company logo**

You'd better make them memorable. And you better make the quick.

A note about e-mail. If you're a company of any size at all, meaning more than just you being a Lone Ranger at your desk in your den, get a real e-mail address. None of this Hotmail or AOL crap. Those accounts should be for personal use, not for professional communication. If you want your company to look like it's going to be around for more than three months, get yourself a domain name for your website and for your employees' addresses. It's a minimal and worthwhile investment in your business.

Respond with a personal surprise. After I wrote an article on getting your foot in the door, Sheila Neisler, of A Basket O' Carolina, wanted to tell me that a gift basket was a good tool, so she hand-delivered one with personalized items – including a book of quotes on winning and cat food (for Lito). She was talked about in my office for weeks and we developed a lasting business relationship – because she dared to be memorable.

Free Git✗Bit...**Want to know the elements that you can incorporate into a memorable marketing campaign?** Go to www.gitomer.com, register if you're a first-time visitor, and enter the words MEMORABLE MARKETING in the GitBit box.

Do something that says, 'I took the time to get to know you AND I'm acknowledging my appreciation for your business.'

– Jeffrey Gitomer

THE SALES BIBLE

Part 2
Preparing to WOW! the Prospect

The Book of Questions

2.2

Why ask "Why?"

Question:
- How do you build rapport?
- How do you determine prospect needs?
- How do you establish buyer confidence?

Answer: Question.

The idea of asking and answering questions is the heart of a sales presentation.

Without questions, you'll have no answers.

Without answers, you'll have no sales.

Without sales, you'll have no money.

Any questions?

The question is the most important skill
a salesperson should master.
The importance of asking one properly
lies somewhere between sale and no sale.

To sell or not to sell, that is the (power) question.

Two of the most important aspects of selling are asking questions and listening. The proper questions will make the prospect tell you everything you need to sell him or her.

Combine powerful questions with effective listening skills and you will have the power and self-discipline to uncover facts/needs, then formulate a response that moves the buyer to a decision.

Man, that sounds so simple. So why doesn't everyone buy when you try to sell them? Because...

1. You're not doing an effective job of asking questions.

2. You're not doing an effective job of listening to the prospect.

3. You have a preconceived notion about the prospect – prejudging the type of person, anticipating answers, and interrupting dialogue.

4. You think you already know all the answers, so why bother asking questions or listening with full attention?

4.5. You have not uncovered the true needs of the prospect. How can you satisfy needs if you don't know what they are?

The most effective sales call is 25% questioning/talking and 75% listening. How does that compare with what you do? *"Oh, that doesn't apply to me,"* you say. *"My product is different. I need to talk more."* Bull-blank. That's just an excuse. What you're really saying is, *"I don't know how to ask a question effectively."*

How do you ask a question? In a word – open-ended. Avoid *yes* or *no* questions unless you're sure yes is a slam dunk.

Developing and asking power questions is the fulcrum point of your ability to understand the prospect's needs.

Here are 12.5 challenges to the types and styles of questions you ask:

1. IS THE QUESTION CLEAR AND CONCISE? Does the prospect understand the question – and its meaning, content, and implication?

2. DOES THE QUESTION REQUIRE PRODUCTIVE THINKING BEFORE THE PROSPECT CAN FORMULATE A RESPONSE? Have you put the prospect on the path toward your product or service as a result of the question?

3. DOES THE QUESTION FORCE THE PROSPECT TO EVALUATE NEW INFORMATION OR CONCEPTS? Are you building prospect credibility by asking superior questions that don't make people feel inferior, but do challenge them in a new way?

4. DOES THE QUESTION MAKE YOU SEEM MORE KNOWLEDGEABLE THAN YOUR COMPETITORS? Are you separating yourself from the competition by asking questions the competition never thought to ask?

5. DOES THE QUESTION LEAD THE PROSPECT (AND YOU) TO DRAW FROM PAST EXPERIENCE? Are you asking prospects questions that make them share things they are proud of? *These are not only sales questions; they are rapport-building questions.*

6. DOES THE QUESTION GENERATE A RESPONSE THAT THE PROSPECT HAS NEVER THOUGHT OF BEFORE? New twists make you seem different, better, and at the top of your game.

7. DOES THE QUESTION PROVIDE A TIE-DOWN ANSWER THAT MOVES THE PRESENTATION PROCESS CLOSER TO A CLOSE? Using question lead-in or ending words, like *don't you, isn't it, shouldn't you, doesn't it,* provides you with the opportunity for the prospect to say *yes* to a particular part of your presentation and move on to the next area.

8. DOES THE QUESTION RELATE DIRECTLY TO THE PROSPECT'S (BUSINESS) SITUATION? The more direct the question, the more likely you are to get a direct response.

9. DOES THE QUESTION RELATE DIRECTLY TO THE PROSPECT'S OBJECTIVES? Are you probing in areas that the prospect can relate to? Areas that make the prospect commit to real answers?

10. DOES THE QUESTION DRAW INFORMATION FROM THE PROSPECT THAT HELPS YOU MAKE THE SALE EASIER? Questions relating to his or her expectations about how your product or service will be used.

11. DOES THE QUESTION CREATE AN ATMOSPHERE THAT IS POSITIVE AND CONDUCIVE TO MAKE A SALE? Is the question provocative or provoking? Don't make prospects mad when you ask a question – make them think.

12. ARE YOU ASKING A QUESTION BACK WHEN A PROSPECT ASKS YOU ONE? Prospect: *Can I get delivery in two weeks?* Salesperson: *Is that when you need it delivered?*

12.5 THE ULTIMATE QUESTION – ARE YOU ASKING A CLOSING QUESTION? A question to which the answer confirms the sale.

Do you have 10 or 12 different closing questions written down to rehearse and use as the occasion arises? I bet you don't.

Want to master the science of formulating and asking power questions? Here's what to do. Write two or three questions that respond to each of the 12.5 challenges above and incorporate them into your selling process.

When you do, you'll discover that it's a challenging task. But the reward for doing it is you will become a better, more financially rewarded salesperson – forever.

> Questions are to sales as breath is to life. If you fail to ask them, you will die. If you ask them incorrectly, your death won't be immediate, but it's inevitable. If you ask them correctly, the answer will be … a sale.

Free GitBit...**Want to learn a three-level strategy for setting up and asking the question that could change the way you make sales?** Go to www.gitomer.com, register if you're a first-time visitor, and enter the words THREE-LEVEL STRATEGY in the GitBit box.

Sales solutions are easy once you identify the prospect's problems, concerns, and needs...
with questions.

Can you close a sale in five questions?

Questions breed sales. Using power questions to find facts is critical to creating an atmosphere in which a sale can be made. Ray Leone, author of *Success Secrets of the Sales Funnel*, issued this challenge: *Can you close a sale in five questions?*

A mixture of Ray's ideas and mind led to this... Sales solutions are easy once you identify the prospect's problems. But that can only occur with well-crafted questions – questions that extract information, needs, and concerns. The sale is most easily made once you *identify the prospect's real needs* and *harmonize with his concerns.*

Let's say I sell printing...

(Have a notepad out and use it as the prospect responds.)

QUESTION ONE: "Mr. Prospect, how do you select a printer?" (Variation: "How do you choose a printer?")

Prospect says, "Quality, delivery, and price."

QUESTION TWO: "How do you define quality?" or "What does quality mean to you?" (Ask the same "How do you define...?" question for all three responses of the "How do you choose...?" question.)

The prospect will give you thoughtful answers. Many prospects have never been asked questions like these and will be forced to think in new patterns. Ask a follow-up question here before going to question three. For example, the prospects says he defines quality as "crisp, clear printing." So you ask, "You mean printing that reflects the image of the quality of your company?" How can a prospect possibly say no to that question?

QUESTION THREE: "What makes that important to you?" or "Is that most important to you?" or "Why is that important to you?"

This question draws out the true need of the prospect. Finding out what is important to them about printing and why printing is important are the keys to closing the sale. There may be secondary or follow-up questions to gain a clear definition of what is important and why.

QUESTION FOUR: "If I could deliver the quality you demand so that the image in your printing reflects the image of your business to your customers, and I could do it in the time frame you require, at a reasonable [not the cheapest] price, would I be [variation: is there any reason I would not be] a candidate for your business?"

Of course you would! This is a feedback question that combines the data found in the first three questions. It's the classic "If I... would you?" question that makes the prospect commit. It actually quasi-closes the prospect. If there's a true objection (We have to get bids. Someone else decides. I'm satisfied with my present vendor.), it's likely to surface here.

QUESTION FIVE: "Great! When could we begin?" or "Great! When is your next printing project?"

The object of the fifth question is to pin the prospect down to a beginning date or time or quantity to start doing business. In many cases you can sell a sample order or trial. Where big-ticket products are involved (copiers, computers), a puppy dog approach will work best (leave your product for the customer to use for a few days), or take the prospect to visit a loyal customer and see your product in operation and get a live testimonial.

Use the questioning process early and often. If you're doing a lot of talking and the prospects are not, you're boring the prospects and losing the sale. They don't care what you've got unless it serves their needs. The only way to identify those needs is to ask 'em.

To use questions successfully, they must be thought out and written down in advance. Develop a list of 15 to 25 questions that uncover needs, problems, pains, concerns, and objections. Develop 15 to 25 more that create prospect commitment as a result of the information you have uncovered.

Looking for a few additional power question lead-ins? Try these...

- What do you look for...?
- What have you found...?
- How do you propose...?
- What has been your experience...?
- How have you successfully used...?
- How do you determine...?
- Why is that a deciding factor...?
- What makes you choose...?
- What do you like about...?
- What is one thing you would improve about...?
- What would you change about...?
  (Do not say, "What don't you like about...?")
- Are there other factors...?
- What does your competitor do about...?
- How do your customers react to...?

Practice. After about 30 days of asking the right questions, you'll begin to see the real rewards.

TAKE HEART: This is not hard sell. It's heart sell.

"Good questions get to the heart of the problem or need very quickly without the buyer feeling like he or she is being pushed."

– *Jeffrey Gitomer*

The Book of Power

Income Statement

A power statement is electric with selling energy.

Are you energizing prospects with words of power. Or are your batteries dead?

Are you putting them to sleep or knocking them out?

Do you make a memorable impact on your prospects?

You better.

You can be sure you do when you use Power Statements.

Your brain is your power tool. Plug it in.

Turn your current into currency with your creative power.

Power statements make your product
or service outstanding, credible,
understandable, and buyable.

You are now under my power (statement).

WHAT IS A POWER STATEMENT? It's a statement that makes your product or service outstanding, understandable, credible, INCREDIBLE, and buyable. It's a non-traditional statement that describes what you do and how you do it in terms of the customer and their perceived use or need for what you're selling.

WHERE DOES THE STATEMENT GET ITS POWER? Your creativity.

You're trying to make a sale or the impact that leads to one. The objective is to persuade and motivate the prospect or customer to act. *That's what a power statement is designed to do.* If you do it right, it also distances you from – and sets you above – your competition.

How do you create a power statement for your business? *Easy* – just think of what you do in terms of how your customer will benefit. Not a boring description, but a vivid, alliterative, benefit-filled picture – an energetic group of words that has the prospect wanting more.

Here's the mind-set needed for generating power statements:

- **Don't sell drill bits.** Sell the perfectly smooth holes they create.
- **Don't sell printing.** Sell the brochures that will reflect your prospect's image and impact her sales.
- **Don't sell cars.** Sell the prestige and status you'll have, or the smooth ride.
- **Don't sell insurance.** Sell safe, financially-secure families protected from tragedy.
- **Don't sell eyeglasses.** Sell better vision and a stylish look.

Power statements have several purposes and can serve many needs in completing and solidifying the sale.

A power statement:

- **Makes a prospect think about what you do in terms of how he or she can use what you offer.**
- **Builds your credibility with a prospect.**
- **Describes what you do and how you do it – in terms of the benefits to your prospect.**
- **Draws a clear line of distinction between you and your competitor.**
- **Makes the prospect want to hear more.**
- **Gives the customer a reason to buy.**
- **Breaks down resistance.**
- **Makes a more favorable impact on the prospect.**
- **Links what you do and how it relates to the prospect.**
- **Is memorable.**
- **Creatively says what you do in terms of the prospect's needs.**

How do you respond when someone ask you what you do? I'll bet it's a boring, one-sentence description that has the other person looking for someone else to talk to.

Here are some examples of how to use a power statement instead of the previous answer you gave to the question What do you do?...

- **TEMPORARY HELP:** I provide quality emergency and temporary employees for businesses like yours so that when one of your own employees is sick, absent, or on vacation, there is no loss of productivity or reduction of service to your customers.

- **MEN'S CLOTHING:** My experience has shown that salespeople dress for their customers. I create the look you need to make that important presentation. *Variation:* Bruce Julian at Milton's Clothing Cupboard in Charlotte has a great power statement: "When my customers have an important meeting or speech to make, they go to their closet and select clothing they bought at Milton's." *WOW!*

POWER STATEMENTS ARE MEMORABLE OPENING LINES. I went to one of those business opportunity (franchise) shows. Companies trying to sell businesses for $10,000 to $150,000. There were more than 100 businesses represented. Half were immediately recognizable by their national stature.

I took my recorder because I was sure I would hear dozens of gems. *Wrong, franchise breath.* They were disappointing (pathetic). After the first twenty or so duds, I was hoping to find one gem. I did. As I walked by a booth loaded with Mickey Mouse products and clothing, a woman met me in the aisle and said, "Mickey Mouse makes more money in a year than every company in this room, combined!" Wow, what a line. I thanked her for making my day. She gave me a puzzled "You're welcome?"

Power statements generate interest and get appointments:

- **Generic-interest power statement:** Your key to profits is productivity. Last year we grew sales by more than 300% by providing items that arrived on time and aided our customer's productivity. In 30 days we can improve yours.

- **Generic appointment power statement:** I'm not sure if I can help you, Mr. Johnson. Let me explore some details with you for a few minutes (or over lunch). If I think I can help you, I'll tell you, and if I think I can't, I'll tell you that, too. Fair enough?

HAVE YOU CREATED YOUR POWER STATEMENTS YET? Create your power statements now. Get out a sheet of paper in your sales meeting. Brainstorm them with your sales team. Bring in your most powerful salesperson – your president. Write your power statements for all situations. Why not take a fresh, powerful look at your selling expressions?

Power statements are a great way to sell against the competition. Overpower them!

The Book
of
Introductions

Shake!

Introductions...

Do they listen
to your pitch
with a friendly ear,
or pitch you out
on your rear?

Are you a sales professional
or a professional visitor?

You've got a few precious
minutes to make a
powerful and professional
first impression.

If you can't open,
you can't close.

Knock, knock...

3.1

Your commercial is an opportunity to provide information that creates interest and response from people you network with.

The 30-second personal commercial – how to write it.

When you go to a business meeting or are networking, you're on the lookout for contacts and prospects.

Your personal commercial (also known as an elevator speech or cocktail commercial) is an opportunity to provide information that creates interest and response from prospects. It is the prelude and the gateway to a sale.

How effective is your commercial? Do you even have one?

YOUR OBJECTIVE IS TO HAVE THIRTY SECONDS OF INFORMATION. Thirty seconds that states who you are and what company you represent, and creatively tells what you do.

AFTER YOU SAY A LITTLE – ASK A LOT. Ask one (or a series of) power questions that engages. Make a power statement that tells how you can help others. And end with why the prospect should act now.

The information you gain from your power questions will allow you to formulate an impact response to show that you can help. The questions must be open-ended questions, questions that get the prospect thinking and talking, not just saying yes or no.

There is no reason to tell a prospect how you can help until you have uncovered what kind of help they need.

The power question is the most critical part of the process because it qualifies the prospect, sets up your impact (power) response, and makes the prospect think.

When formulating your power questions for your commercial, ask yourself these 4.5 questions:

1. **What information do I want to get as a result of asking this question?**

2. **Can I qualify my prospect as a result of the question?**

3. **Does it take more than one question to find out the information I need?**

4. **Do my questions make the prospect think?**

4.5 **Can I ask a question that separates me from my competitor?**

You should have a list of 25 power questions that make the prospect stop and think and give you the information you need to strike. The closure of your 30-second commercial should be a call to action – a closing line, statement, or question that ensures another contact.

Here's an example of a personal commercial:

Let's say you're out with a customer networking at her trade association meeting and she introduces you to a prospect. The prospect says, "What do you do?" If you're in the temporary staffing industry and you say, "I'm in the temporary staffing industry," you should be fired.

Your reply should be, "I provide quality emergency and temporary employees to businesses like yours so that when one of your employees is sick, absent, or on vacation, there is no loss of productivity or reduction of service to your customers." *Deliver a line like that, and the person you're speaking with can't help but be impressed.*

Now that you have the prospect's attention, ask your power questions to find out how qualified the person is.

"How many employees do you have?" you ask. "Do you give them one week or two weeks of vacation?" "How do you ensure that the level of service to your customers isn't reduced during those vacation times?"

Continue to ask more follow-up questions until you get the information you need. After your power questions, insert your power statement (how you help) and a reason why the prospect should act now.

"I specialize in smart, capable people. Not temporary help. When your people are on vacation, or out sick, I know you can't afford low morale or a reduction in service. Here's what I propose: (This is your call to action statement and the reason your prospect should act now.) Let's meet for breakfast and discuss your last few employee absences. We'll talk about how they were handled and discuss the next few upcoming absences. If I think I can help you, I'll tell you. And if I don't think I can help you, I'll tell you that, too. Is that fair enough?"

Use this example to help you write your own personal commercial. After you write it, rehearse it. Then, go try it out and adjust it for the real world.

Then, practice it (more than 25 times in real situations) until you own it.

Your personal commercial worksheet:

INSTRUCTIONS: Fill out this two-page form. Read it from top to bottom. Add a few personal pronouns. Time it. Practice it. Study it. And voilá!

My name: _____

My company name: _____

What I do: _____

_____

_____

My power questions: _____

_____

_____

_____

My power statement: _____

_____

_____

_____

How can I help: _____

_____

_____

_____

Why should the prospect act now: _____

_____

_____

_____

*"Before we begin our meeting, let's swap contact lenses.
It might help us see things from each other's point of view!"*

Don't deliver too soon. Wait until you have enough information from the prospect before you strike.

The 30-second personal commercial – how to deliver it.

You just wrote your personal commercial and now it's time to deliver it. Think of delivering your personal business commercial as a pitcher would throw in a baseball game. You want to make a pitch that's a strike, but all batters are not alike. They require different types of pitches – fast ball, curve, slider, and the ever-popular screwball. (Isn't it amazing how many screwballs we pitch?)

In order to pitch to the batter most effectively, you need to know what type of hitter he is. You need to know his hitting strengths and weaknesses. Every baseball team has a "book" on every other player in the league. They know how to pitch him and where the fielders should play in the event he hits the ball. It is no different in sales. You can't pitch the prospect effectively if you don't know what his needs are. You must know how to play each prospect. It's easy to get a strike in sales. All you have to do is ask your prospects questions. They will be delighted to tell you all about themselves.

Be prepared. When you meet a prospect or a prospect comes up to you, are you ready? Test yourself:

- **What do you want his or her first impression to be? How will you create that?**
- **How quickly can you qualify him or her?**
- **What kind of questions can you ask that will qualify your prospect and generate interest in what you do?**
- **Do you have a list of your Power Questions? Are they rehearsed?**
- **Do you have a list of your Power Statements? Are they rehearsed?**

Here are 9.5 personal commercial delivery commandments...

1. BE BRIEF. Your remarks (other than questions) should be no more than 30 to 60 seconds.

2. BE TO THE POINT. Say something that creatively tells prospects exactly what you do in terms of their needs.

3. BE REMEMBERED. Say, give, or do something creative that will stay in the prospect's mind (in a positive way).

4. BE PREPARED. Have your information at your command – rehearsed, practiced, and polished.

5. HAVE POWER QUESTIONS AND POWER STATEMENTS READY. Prepare a list of questions and statements in advance and rehearse them.

6. GET THE INFORMATION YOU NEED. Ask power and follow-up questions that generate information, establish interest, show need, and allow you to give your information in a meaningful way. Ask your best questions and have your most concise message ready to deliver when the timing is right. Before you explain your problem-solving capabilities, know enough about the other person so that your information has impact.

7. SHOW HOW YOU SOLVE PROBLEMS. The prospect is bored hearing about what you do, unless you tell him in a way that helps or serves him. The prospect doesn't care what you do, unless what you do impacts him.

8. PIN THE PROSPECT DOWN TO THE NEXT ACTION. Don't let a good prospect go without some agreement about what's next.

9. HAVE FUN. Don't press or be pressured – it will show.

9.5 TIME'S UP. When you have delivered your message, made your contact, and secured the next meeting or action – move on.

IMPORTANT: Don't say ANY words that aren't an integral part of your commercial. Be as concise as possible. Be creative. If it drags, no one will listen or be inclined to act. Make your message in terms of the customer (*you, your*), not in terms of you (*me, I*). Be original. Boring messages are forgotten immediately. Say, do, or hand out something that will be remembered. Ask open-ended, thought-provoking questions.

The delivery of your commercial is successfully achieved when you are able to match your services exactly to specifically identified prospect needs. This can only be achieved with excellent preplanning and preparation.

When you get a referral, treat it like gold.

Got a referral?
Here's the perfect approach.

You got it. The most coveted prize in selling besides a sale. A referral. How do you approach this person? How do you maximize the selling power of this referral?

Here are eight rules to ensure your success:

Rule #1: GO SLOW. Timing is everything. Don't appear to be too anxious to get the sale (money). Proper setup (giving some value first) will breed a long-term relationship (more money) instead of just a sale.

Rule #2: ARRANGE A THREE-WAY MEETING. Setting the stage for the first meeting/communication can be make it or break it. All three people (you, the referral, and the person who referred them) together sets a perfect stage. And it's your best chance for success. A third party singing your praise in front of the referral is a HUGE level to the sale. One third-party endorsement is more powerful than 100 presentations.

Rule #3: YOU DON'T HAVE TO SELL AT THE FIRST MEETING IF YOUR CUSTOMER IS WITH YOU. In fact, the less selling you do, the more credible you will appear. You only have to establish rapport to gain confidence from the prospect.

Rule #4: ARRANGE A SECOND, PRIVATE MEETING. This is where you'll get down to business.

Rule #5: DON'T SEND TOO MUCH INFORMATION IN THE MAIL. The mail, like the phone, is not where a sale is made. It's just a sales tool. Send just enough to inform and create interest.

Rule #6: WRITE A PERSONAL NOTE TO THE REFERRAL WITHIN 24 HOURS. Brief but positive. Don't slobber all over the note with thanks, and thanks again. Just tell him or her it was nice to get acquainted and you're looking forward to the next meeting.

Rule #7: WRITE YOUR CUSTOMER A NOTE OF THANKS. Include a gift if the sale will be of some significance (a *quality* ad specialty – something with your logo printed on it, or two tickets to a ball game). Your thanks and gift will encourage the customer to get you another referral.

Rule #8: OVERDELIVER! Failure to follow up and deliver as promised makes you and your customer look bad to the prospect. Failure to deliver also eliminates any chance of another referral. This rule is the most important of them all; it is a breeding ground for your reputation. *What kind of delivery reputation have you got?*

ONE FINAL REAL-WORLD NOTE. The least preferred or least productive way to use a referral, but the way it seems to happen most often, is a stone cold call (or letter) to a name, address, and number given to you by a customer or friend. It is where the referral is lost. PLEASE: Be creative. Make it a meaningful and personal connection. Get some information about the referral and his company before the first contact is made. Don't fall into the trap of calling or writing and saying, *"I was given your name by…"* That sounds horrible.

Say instead, *"Hi, my name is Jeffrey. My company is BuyGitomer, and you don't know me from a sack of potatoes. I've been doing business with [name of customer] for some time now, and she thought I might be able to help you in the same way I've helped her. I just wanted to introduce myself and get your address to send you some information I think you'll find of interest."*

Now say something CREATIVE to establish personal rapport from the information you were given by your customer.

Try to get the referral to laugh. Then say, *"I'll call you back in a few days, and maybe we can talk over lunch. Thanks for your time."*

Don't be too windy. You're not going to make the sale on the phone. Say just enough to create interest and arrange an in-person meeting.

The referral is the easiest prospect in the world to sell. Ask any professional who hates selling (accountants, architects, lawyers) – they'll tell you that 100% of their new business comes from referrals. That's because they're not capable of making sales calls and rely on the fall-in-your-lap method of selling.

"One third-party endorsement is worth a hundred presentations, if you know what you're doing."

— *Jeffrey Gitomer*

The Book of Cold Calling

You don't know me from a sack of potatoes.

Cold calls...

Most everyone hates 'em.
Most everybody makes 'em.

Why not make
the most of 'em?

Have fun at 'em.
Make a game out of 'em.
Play to win.

Every *no* gets you
closer to *yes*.

3.2

What do salespeople think
of No Soliciting signs?

"No Soliciting,"
the funniest sign in sales.

I have a sign on my company's front door that says *Solicitors Welcome.*

But it seems every office building I go into has a sign on the door that says, *No Soliciting.* It has to be the funniest sign in sales. What a useless sign to post in front of a salesman. I'd like to have a dollar for every "No Soliciting" sign I've ignored. What is the purpose of this sign and whom does it deter?

It's interesting to me that many of the businesses that sport the sign have cold calling salespeople themselves. It's somewhat hypocritical to see *No Soliciting* on the door of a copier business, insurance broker, or temporary help agency.

What do salespeople think of *No Soliciting* signs? I polled the Early Risers Lead Club, the largest pure sales lead association in the Charlotte area, made up of entrepreneurs and salespeople. I asked how they felt and what they did when they encountered the dreaded sign. Out of 32 people, only two said they would respect the sign; two said they have fear but enter anyway; 28 (87.5%) said they ignore it. It's also interesting to note that the same salespeople think it's okay to ban the door-to-door peddlers selling candy, perfume, and pictures. You know, solicitors.

SECRET: It seems that salespeople from legitimate businesses believe that the sign is not aimed at them. I agree.

I was having a discussion with a company president and his sales manager. They've adopted a new policy NOT to screen incoming cold calls. They feel that too many opportunities are missed by not listening to what a salesperson has to offer or say. What a great way to think! Of course, as a sales warrior, you've known that all along.

*To find out who decides,
make a passive statement
and ask an indirect question.
"I've got some important information
about new computers. Who should I leave it for?"*

Get to the decision maker on a cold call.

Getting past the *No Soliciting* sign is easy. It's getting to the decision maker that requires skill and finesse. If you use the line, "I'd like to speak with the boss," it will never get you to the boss without a major hassle. Don't ask to speak to anyone.

The key to getting to a decision maker is to make an indirect and nonassertive request for "information only" from the secretary or administrative person. He or she will gladly give you all the facts you need to make the perfect follow-up.

LET'S SAY YOU'RE SELLING COMPUTERS: "I need your help. My name is Jeffrey, and I've got some important information about computers. Who should I leave it for (or send it to, if calling)?" If you get the name, you MUST ask the following double-confirming questions: "Is she the person who decides on this type of thing? Is there anyone else who works with her on this type of decision?"

If the front-desk person says, "Just leave the information with me," ask him or her politely, "Are you the person who decides on computers?" They will usually back off quickly. If they don't, you must still be as nice as pie in requesting the all-important decider's name.

Be gentle but persistent until you get the name. You may have to try three or four approaches. Don't quit until you get the name and ask the double-confirming questions.

Here's how to handle a No Soliciting *sign and get to the decision maker...*

I cold called every office in every (*No Soliciting*) office building in uptown Charlotte. I got off at the top floor and worked my way down each tower. I got tossed out of two offices. One actually called the sales police. *But they can only throw you out into the hallway!* You, of course, promise not to do it again, get on the elevator, get off at the next floor, and keep on cold calling. *No Soliciting* is actually more of a game than a rule.

The sign is meant for door-to-door-type sales crews who canvass an area trying to sell handbags, perfume, calculators, and wall hangings. If you have a legitimate, established business, making a cold call will not be offensive to most businesses *if you do it right.* The best method is an *indirect solicitation* – dropping off literature and asking a few questions.

If you're out making an appointed sales call, it's a great use of time to make a few *next-door neighbor* cold calls after that appointment. I always do. If there's a *No Soliciting* sign, I don't even think about it. The entire cold call process takes less than five minutes.

Here are the guidelines to follow to ensure maximum No Soliciting *success:*

1. **Ignore the sign.**
2. **Have literature and business cards.**
3. **Ask for help.**
4. **Get the name and title of the decision maker.**
5. **Write him or her a personalized note on your business card, attach it to your information, and ask for your package to be delivered ASAP.**
6. **Ask for (and get) the decision maker's card.**
7. **Find out when is the best time to call the decision maker.**
8. **Get the name of the person who helped you, and write it down on the back of the decider's card.**
9. **Thank the person genuinely for their help.**
9.5 **Leave.** *Try this pitch next time...*

"Hi, my name is Jeffrey and I was wondering if you could help me. (Everyone wants to help.) I want to leave some valuable information about my product/service. Who decides on that type of thing?"
"Oh, that would be Mr. Johnson," she gleefully volunteers.

Great, now I know the decision maker, but I'm going to double qualify while I'm on a roll. "What would his position be?" I query innocently. You'll get that answer, too. "Is there anyone else he works with on this type of decision?" I'm asking to find out if I've reached the biggest person. If I get questioned, I simply say, "I usually mail two packages of information if there are two people involved in the decision." That usually shuts the gatekeeper up.

Now I make a bold move. "I'm leaving this information and a note for him. I wonder if I could get his card." You'll get the card 90% of the time; 5% you'll get some facsimile of the card; and 5% of the time the boss himself will appear. If you're a female salesperson and the boss is male, the boss will appear twice as often. That's not a sexist remark; that's a fact.

"When would be the best time to call him?" I ask, trying to get the last bit of info before I wear out my uninvited welcome.

"Thank you so much for helping me. I really appreciate it," I say. "What was your name?" "Thank you, Susan."

People love to hear their name associated with praise and thanks. If you do both, she'll remember you the next time you call and need to speak to Mr. Johnson.

Look at all the information you got! You may not have made a money sale the first time, but they bought your pitch and you're loaded for bear on the next call. *Check out your prizes for being nice and nonpushy...*

1. **The decision maker's name and card.**

2. **Whether he or she acts alone.**

3. **The decision maker has your information.**

4. **He or she has your card and personal note.**

5. **You made friends with the secretary.**

5.5 **You know the best time to call back.**

My follow up call will be made 24 hours later, and Susan will help me every way she can. Now all I need is an appointment, a contract, and a check.

*Good or bad, your opening line
will immediately establish an impression.
It sets the tone for the sale.*

Opening is as important as closing.

On a sales call, your professionalism and your friendliness are the first things a customer or prospect sees. Then comes the impact of that all-important first line. *Your delivery, sincerity, and creativity set the tone for the rest of the conversation.* They also determine how the prospect listens. If you get attention and respect, you're likely to keep it throughout. If not, you're likely to leave empty handed.

If you're on the phone, the opening line is even more important. It's all you've got. You can't say, "Look at my nice suit." You're at the mercy of (or the mastery of) your words.

Here are 7.5 rules to follow for cold calling on the phone:

1. **Smile when you talk.**

2. **Give your name and company.**

3. **Get to the point fast (state your purpose within the first two sentences).**

4. **Make it short and sweet.**

5. **Try to be somewhat humorous.**

6. **Offer or ask for help.**

7. **State that you have important information.**

7.5 **Ask for the sale. The "sale" may only be to get an appointment. But whatever your objective was when you picked up the phone ... persist until you get it.**

Use the same rules for cold phone calling and select from the following:

1. **I've been thinking about what you do.**

2. **I've got the answer to your question.**

3. **I've got some important information that will impact your business.**

A majority of salespeople make the fatal mistake of asking, "Did you get the information I sent you?" If the prospect says *no*, what do you say now, genius? You can fumble about how you sent it three days ago and how you can't understand how that could have happened, but that's lame, sounds defensive, and you have ruined any chances of making a positive call.

Try saying this instead: "I'm calling about the information I sent. *It wasn't completely self-explanatory,* and I'd like an opportunity to discuss it with you personally for about 5 to 10 minutes."

If you want to gain immediate benefit from reading this today, make a list of the opening lines you use in your business, revise them, analyze them closely, and compare them with those of your co-workers. Try out your revised lines tomorrow. The results will surprise (and benefit) you.

"I don't have any sales experience, but I think
I'd be very good at making cold calls!"

If you use humor and get a blank stare,
you're dead.
But a cold call is a crapshoot anyway.
Why not have fun?

The cold call is fun.
If you think it is.

Cold calling is one reason many people shy away from a career in sales. Sales professionals who make a six-figure income will tell you that cold call training provided the basis for their sales success. Doubt it? Ask 'em.

Here is an 8-point game plan to begin succeeding at cold calling:

1. BE EXCEPTIONALLY WELL PREPARED. Know your best targets (preplan). Have a purpose (the big picture). Know your objective (get an appointment, get a name). Have a memorized script (lines, power lines, power questions). Have perfect materials and tools (something of value for the prospect).

2. DON'T APOLOGIZE FOR ANYTHING, DON'T MAKE EXCUSES. When you get there, get to your business. Don't say, "I'm sorry to interrupt." Just deliver your line.

3. HOW YOU DELIVER YOUR FIRST LINE DETERMINES YOUR SUCCESS. The impact of the first sentence will determine success or failure.

4. DON'T PAY ANY ATTENTION TO RELUCTANCE OR FEAR ISSUES. Cold call reluctance is another way of saying, *"I don't know how"* or *"I can't plan"* or *"I don't like it when people reject me."* Develop a pitch, read positive books, stop watching the news, and believe you can succeed.

5. NOT EVERYONE YOU CALL IS A SALE. BE PREPARED FOR REJECTION. People aren't rejecting you, they're only rejecting the offer you're making them. *There, that feels better, doesn't it?*

6. LEARN FROM THOSE WHO TELL YOU NO. Find out what caused them to say no or not be interested.

7. PRACTICE, PRACTICE, PRACTICE. Unless you own your pitch, you'll sound contrived. Nothing's worse than a salesperson sounding like a salesperson.

8. HAVE FUN! You're being paid to get the sales education of a lifetime. It ain't brain cancer; it's a sales call. Have a good time. Make someone smile.

8.5 IF YOU SAY, "*I HATE COLD CALLS!*" REALIZE IT IS A SELF-INDUCED MENTAL STATE THAT IS EASILY OVERCOME BY A SERIES OF COLD CALL SUCCESSES, SALES, AND COMMISSIONS.

Here is a personalized formula to help you get better at cold calling:

- **Identify your weaknesses and fears about cold calls. List them in detail.**
- **Create an action plan for weaknesses so that you can overcome and eliminate them one by one.**
- **Work on one every 30 days.**
- **Challenge yourself to succeed every day.**
- **Quit complaining. No one buys from a complainer.**

Three of the most important parts of the cold call are opening lines, *power questions*, and *power statements*. They allow you to gather information needed to determine the prospect's real needs.

Two more parts are *attitude* and *focus*. Positive attitude will impact the prospect, and proper focus permits you to use your skills to create action.

And the most important part of the cold call is *ask for the sale.*

Free Git✗Bit...**Want some examples of good and bad opening lines?** Go to www.gitomer.com, register if you're a first-time visitor, and enter the word OPENERS in the GitBit box.

*Prospects are just as motivated to avoid
losing something they already have
as they are to buy something new.*

Elements of a cold call that can make it hot.

Cold calling is one of the most difficult parts of selling. An old sales cliché says that the hardest door for a salesman to open is the car door.

To be successful at the science of cold calling, you must first define the elements, functions, and formulas that comprise the call. Then, like all other sciences, experiment (practice) until you have a method that works.

The basic elements that comprise a cold call are:

1. **Say a few words.**
2. **Ask Power (thought-provoking) Questions to create meaningful dialogue.**
3. **Make Power (benefit) Statements to establish credibility.**
4. **Qualify the prospect as to need, desire, decision-making capability, and money (the ability to pay).**
5. **Gather information.**
6. **Get what you came for – or at least secure the next step in your sales cycle.**
6.5 **Have the right attitude and focus to accept either yes or no.**

Here are several cold calling elements, guidelines, and ideas that have proven to be effective:

• **Opening lines are important.** Deliver a smooth, sincere line. Say you're a single woman and a guy comes up to you in some social circumstance and says, "Don't I know you?" or "You're just the prettiest little thing I ever did see." The first thing you think is, "This guy's a jerk. Get me out of here." It's the same in cold calling. The opening line determines if you get to dance.

- **Opening impressions are important.** The way you look and come across in the first 30 seconds often (not always) determines your outcome.

- **After you deliver the opener, make the prospect think.** Your questions (*Power Questions*) and statements (*Power Statements*) are critical to gaining prospect confidence. Ask questions that show knowledge, imply prospect areas of weakness, and gather vital information. Make statements that are creatively descriptive, imply benefits, and build your credibility.

- **Get to the point fast.** The prospect is busy and will be insulted if you beat around the bush.

- **If you are asked for a price, give it immediately.** Try to do it in the most creative way you can, but give it.

- **Determine what your prospects need.** By understanding the problems of their operation, appealing to their sense of greed, evoking their fears, appealing to their vanity, determining what their customer needs, and finding (searching for) their hot button – and pushing it.

- **They will resist you.** So what? It takes seven exposures, seven tries to get the prospect to become a customer. If you quit after just one or two, the sale will go to the next guy/woman who shows up.

- **They will buy to solve a business problem or satisfy a need.** Statements and questions need to be pointed in that direction. Stress benefits (what's in it for them), not features (how it works). Emphasize what they will gain – profit, pride, reputation. Prove that they will avoid pain, loss, criticism. *Failure to express benefits in terms of customer needs will preclude the sale.*

- **Focus on *negative prevention.*** Get them to share what dissatisfies them. Motivate them to show discontent with their current situation. Tell them how they'll safeguard profits, eliminate worry, overcome fear, and avoid the terror of *customer complaints.* Prospects are just as motivated to avoid losing something they already have as they are to buy something new.

- **Gain buyer confidence.** Use every weapon in your sales-tool arsenal. Bring in testimonials, references, and similar situations whenever possible.

- **Attitude, humor, and action (persistence) will whip fears and rejection. Fear of failure doesn't exist if you believe it doesn't.** You will be rejected – the prospect will reject your offer – big deal! Edison, Lincoln, Babe Ruth, Colonel Sanders – these guys failed miserably thousands of times. Where would they be without their attitude to succeed? (And where would we be without their successes?) ***You only fail when you quit!***

- **Set your own goals for achievement.** How many calls per day, how many appointments per day. Selling is a numbers game, but it will only work if you are prepared. You must work your numbers consistently to get them to pay. Push yourself to win. If you cold call enough people, you will make appointments (your objective), and you will make sales (your purpose).

"You're now armed
with enough cold
calling knowledge to
choke a horse.
Don't let it get
to your throat."

— *Jeffrey Gitomer*

The Book of Presentations

On with the show, this is it!

Presentations…

Overture: hit the lights.
Now's your chance.
Get it right.

Can you tell the prospect
what he wants to hear?
Is he even listening?
Does he take you seriously?

Can you motivate him to
act?
Can you give him enough
confidence to buy?
Or are you a one-act play?

Want your prospects
to scream:
Bravo! Encore!

Two minutes to curtain…

If you can establish common ground
with your prospects, they will like you,
trust you, and buy from you.

Want to make the sale easier?
Establish prospect rapport first.

What do you do to establish rapport? Are you sharp enough to find something besides business after you open the conversation? Here are some ideas you can try on the phone, at the prospect's place of business, at your place of business, or at a networking event.

ON THE PHONE: *It's likely that you're calling to make an appointment, so focus on 3.5 things:*

    1. **Get to the point in 15 seconds.**

    2. **Be happy and humorous.**

    3. **Get to know something personal about the prospect.**

  3.5 **Nail down the appointment.**

You first begin to establish rapport by getting to the point! State the purpose of your call immediately. It's not necessary (and it's often a put-off) to ask the insincere "How are you today?" Just state your name, your company name, and how you can help the prospect. Once you've done that, there is a sense of relief on both sides. The prospect is relieved because he now knows why you've called, and you're relieved because the prospect hasn't hung up on you. Now you can go about the task of establishing some rapport and setting the appointment.

Try to use humor at least twice during the conversation (but don't force it). People love to laugh. A quick, clean 10-second joke can do more for buyer rapport than 10 minutes worth of sales talk.

You can gain insight by listening. Prospect mood, hometown, and personality will all be revealed in just a few minutes on the phone. I listen closely for speech accent. It gives me a clue about where my prospect hails from – a great subject if you're well traveled or come from the same place.

Listen for and be sensitive to the mood of the prospect. If he or she is noticeably short or gruff, just say, "I can tell you're busy [or, 'not having the best of days']. Why don't we pick a time more convenient for me to call?"

If you know the prospect, you can sell the appointment with a personal touch. For example, if you're talking to a basketball fan, you might say, "I know I can help you reach your computer training needs. With a 10-minute appointment I can show you how I can help you in the first five minutes and have the other five to discuss who the Sixers should draft."

Remember, people love to talk about themselves. Getting people to talk about themselves will give you a chance to find common ground, establish rapport, and increase your chance of making the sale.

Establish prospect rapport before you begin your pitch. The best way to win the sale is to first win the prospect. If you find common subjects or interests with a prospect, you can establish a business friendship. People are more likely to buy from a friend than a salesman.

What do you do to establish rapport? Are you observant enough to find something besides business to open the conversation? Here are some ideas:

ON AN APPOINTMENT IN THE PROSPECT'S OFFICE: This is the easiest place to establish rapport. Look for clues as soon as you walk into the prospect's place of business. Pictures, plaques, or awards on the wall; magazines subscribed to that don't match the business. When you get in the prospect's office, look for pictures of children or events, bookcase items, books, diplomas, awards, desk items, or anything that reveals personal likes and/or leisure pursuits. Ask about an award or trophy. Ask about a diploma or picture. Your prospect will be glad to talk about what he or she has accomplished or likes to do.

Try to engage prospects in intelligent conversation with open-ended questions about their interests. It's obviously better if you're well versed in the subject, but the point is to get prospects to talk about what makes them happy. Use humor. Humor builds rapport because it constitutes agreement (when the prospect laughs). Getting the prospect to laugh will set the stage for a positive presentation.

WHEN THE PROSPECT COMES TO YOUR PLACE OF BUSINESS: When your prospective customer comes to your place of business, it is more difficult to establish common ground because you don't have the advantage of the telling items that would be present in his or her surroundings. So, be observant. Look at clothing, car, rings, imprinted items, their business card, or anything that gives you a clue as to the type of person they are.

Be friendly. Ask open-ended questions. Try to find out what they did last weekend, or what they're doing this weekend. Ask about a movie or television show. Avoid politics and their personal problems. And don't lament about your personal problems.

People love to talk about themselves. Ask the right question and it's tough to shut them up. Your objective is to find a subject, idea, or situation that you BOTH know about or are interested in.

Be real. It's as easy to spot an insincere salesperson as a skunk in your living room. Both smell awful.

One word of caution: Be aware of time. The time you're permitted to spend building rapport has a lot to do with where you live geographically. In the Northeast, you may have as little as 30 seconds. In these situations I try to be direct immediately. Gain interest first. Then go for some rapport. In the South, Midwest, Southwest, and West, you can spend 5 to 10 minutes establishing rapport. Don't lose sight of your mission, but, I can assure you the mission is most likely to be accomplished if you make a friend before making a presentation. The key is getting prospects to talk about themselves. This will give you a chance to find common ground, establish rapport, and increase your chance to make a sale.

No rapport, No sale!

Free GitBit...**Want 14.5 get-real questions about establishing buyer confidence?** Go to www.gitomer.com, register if you're a first-time visitor, and enter the words BUYER CONFIDENCE in the GitBit box.

Buyer confidence must be established
by using sales tools, examples, and stories
the prospect can relate to.

12.5 ways to make the prospect confident enough to buy.

Prospects won't buy if they lack confidence in you or your product.

Here are the 12.5 most effective ideas to establish buyer confidence:

1. Be completely prepared. A fumbling, excuse-making, apologizing salesperson builds zero confidence.

2. Involve prospects early in the presentation. Get them to help you or hold your samples. Something that makes them feel like they're on your team.

3. Have something in writing. An article about your company or product from a natioanl news source will reek of credibility.

4. Tell a story or show a video describing how you helped another customer. This creates a similar situation that the prospect can relate to.

5. Use a referral source if possible. "Mr. Prospect, you should call [name of company and contact name] to find out how we helped them."

6. Drop names of larger customers or the buyer's competitors. If you are doing business with a large firm, state it in a way that shows strength and competence rather than sounding like you're bragging.

7. Have a printed list of loyal customers. Include large and small accounts. Make perfect copies on good-quality paper.

8. Have a notebook of testimonial letters. Try to get letters that cover various aspects of your business: quality, delivery, competence, service, and extra effort. Be sure some of your letters answer the buyer's objections.

9. Don't bombard the prospect. Work your examples in as a natural part of the presentation. Let confidence build to a natural close.

10. Emphasize service after the sale. The buyer needs to be certain you won't sell and run. Talk delivery, training, and service.

11. Emphasize long-term relationships. The customer wants to feel that you will be there to help with problems, new technology, growth, and service. Give your home number.

12. Sell to help, not for commissions. Prospects can smell a greedy salesperson. It's a bad odor.

12.5 The most important link to the process. Ask the right questions. Go back to *The Book of Questions* and read it 10 times.

Use your confidence-building tools as you would use trump in a card game. Play it when you need to. If the prospect asks who else uses your product, be prepared with video testimonials.

If your business is relatively new, credibility will be a leading factor in getting the sale. You must sell your personal experience and desire to do a great job.

NOTE: Not once have I mentioned price as a credibility factor. Because it's not. Being the least expensive won't get you anywhere if the prospect has no confidence to buy.

"If you sign the purchase order within 30 seconds, you'll get a 30% discount. If you sign within 25 seconds, you'll get a 25% discount. If you sign within 20 seconds, you'll get a 20% discount. And if you sign tomorrow, there's a price increase!"

"Being the least
expensive won't
get you anywhere if
the prospect has no
confidence to buy.
Many times, low price
actually scares the
buyer."

– Jeffrey Gitomer

Buyer confidence must be
established and reconfirmed
in all phases of the selling process.

Where and when to establish buyer confidence.

The prospects won't buy if they lack confidence in you or your product. Buyer confidence must be established and reconfirmed in all phases of the selling process. Obviously the faster you establish confidence in the selling process, the easier it will be to get to the next phase of the sale.

Here are the prime selling opportunities to establish buyer confidence. Each situation calls for different types of confidence-building ideas:

IN A NETWORKING SITUATION: If you only have time for one statement, make it one that will discuss the use of your product/service by a good company. "We were very fortunate to be awarded the toner cartridge contract from Duke Power. They selected us from among seven other bids." This begins the process of making the prospect feel confident in you.

ON THE PHONE: Use only one item to establish confidence. ***Just sell the appointment.*** For example, "I believe we can help you get the computer training and achieve the productivity you need to cut operating costs. We just completed a similar project for Acme Manufacturing that used the same curriculum. Let me e-mail you a copy of a letter we received from them after the training was completed. I'd like to set up a brief appointment at your office to be certain this curriculum fits your needs exactly." *Your objective is to establish enough confidence to get an appointment – not make a sale.*

ON A COLD CALL: Be brief. You must generate interest in about 30 seconds or less, or forget it. *Make a strong statement about how you can help the prospect.* Don't focus on how much money you can save them. That approach seems to be wearing thin. Talk about what you do for companies like hers, or how your product has worked for others.

If you're not in a *one-call close* business (over 90% are not), you only need to establish enough confidence to make the next appointment.

DURING A PRESENTATION: Save your best stuff for your presentation. Your presentation – either at the prospect's place of business or in your office, is your big chance. Walk in with your bag full of tricks, and use them one by one – like building a brick foundation. Each time the prospect casts a shadow of doubt, have something to counter with that will make you shine. Video testimonials, letters from loyal customers, and articles, examples, and comparison charts that will make the prospect secure enough to buy. Write things down – let the prospect see professional respect for his time and the importance of the meeting. Be confident – confidence begets confidence.

ON A FOLLOW-UP CALL: Relax. Don't sound contrived or forced. If you force it, the prospect will lose the confidence you worked so hard to gain. Have a specific purpose for calling. Use similar situations (good things you've done for others), and specific benefits for the prospect as examples of why he should buy now. *Have lead-in lines prepared:*

- **I was thinking about you.**
- **I was thinking about your business.**
- **Someone paid you a compliment yesterday.**
- **Your name came up in conversation yesterday with.**
- **Something important came up you need to consider.**

How do you know if you have established confidence? Your phone calls are returned. You get the business, or the promise for it.

It's easier to determine you *don't* have the confidence of the prospect. He'll start handing you a bunch of pat-on-the-head responses. "I'll get back to you in a few weeks" or "Our budget is spent" or "I'm not ready to buy yet" or "The board needs to meet and decide." Or, the ever popular, "Call me back in six months." *When you hear stalls, you haven't established enough confidence for the buyer to proceed.*

*The key to being a professional
salesperson is not to sound like one!*

Sales words and phrases to avoid at all costs. Honestly.

Create a new way to ask for the sale.

My friend, Mitchell Kearney (pronounced Carney), is the best commercial photographer in this region. When shooting a subject, he never says, "Smile." That's got to be a major obstacle if you're a photographer. He says it makes him more creative to ask his subject for a smile without ever saying the word. I've looked at hundreds of his photos … most are smiling, so it seems his philosophy works. Mitchell avoids the trite, unimaginative, insincere word that separates the professional from the amateur.

How do you ask your customers to smile and buy today? Are you using words that offend the prospect? Are you using words that create confidence or ruin it? Are you projecting "I'm only here for the order"?

To get the sale, you must use superior word crafting to avoid sounding like an insincere salesperson. If you sound like one, you probably are.

Here are the words and phrases to avoid – forever:

FRANKLY – a word that sounds insincere. All sales courses recommend dropping this word from your vocabulary.

QUITE FRANKLY – a double dose of the dreaded *frankly*. It makes me very suspicious of the person who says it.

HONESTLY – a word that is almost always followed with a lie.

AND I MEAN THAT – No, you don't. This is probably as insincere a phrase as has been turned in the English language.

ARE YOU PREPARED TO ORDER TODAY? – Give me a break. This is an offensive, stupid, turnoff phrase. There are 100 better ways to ask prospects what their feelings are, or when they want to order.

HOW ARE YOU DOING TODAY? – When you hear this on the phone, you immediately think, *What are you selling, jerk?*

CAN I HELP YOU WITH SOMETHING? – The universal anthem of all retail sales clerks. You'd think after 100 years of retail, they might have something more creative and customer service oriented to say.

Here are philosophies to avoid – forever:

Downing the competition – Don't ever. It's not just a no-win situation; it's an absolute losing situation. My mother always told me that if you have nothing nice to say about someone, say nothing. If you down the competition to a prospect, you may be speaking to their relative or spouse, and it makes you look bad.

Preaching ethics – Don't ever say how ethical you are. Let your ethics shine through. The jails are full of televangelists and businesspeople who preached ethics. If you feel you have to prove yourself, use an example of how you performed or responded. Tell the prospect you want a long-term relationship, not just a one-shot order; but don't ever use the word *ethics*. When I hear it in a selling situation, I avoid that person at all costs.

The challenge is for you to rededicate yourself to helping and fulfilling the needs of your customer or prospect. Your creative words and actions (the way you say it and the way you do it) are often the difference between getting a *yes* or *no*. They are the difference between getting the order and letting your main competitor get the order. It's enough to piss you off when your rival gets the business, isn't it? *Well, do something about it.*

How do you do it? You have to work at it. Get co-workers and other salespeople together and work at being different. Talented people in a room will create answers and positive results. Write it down. Practice. And have faith – the results are sure to take you to the bank.

My experience has shown me that if you have to say what you are, you probably aren't. Think about that for a moment. "I'm honest," "I'm ethical," even "I'm the boss," or "I'm in charge," usually indicates just the opposite. Doesn't it?

Prospect involvement
lets them have a sense of ownership
that leads to a purchase.

Physically involving the prospect = more sales.

When I sold franchises in 1972, I drove a big new Cadillac. I would pick up the prospects at their home, and as I walked toward my car, I would say, "Gee, I have a headache, do you mind driving?" By the time Mr. and Mrs. Prospect got to my office, they wanted a car just like mine. They would buy the franchise I was selling to get a Cadillac with the profits they were sure to make. *I involved the prospect in the sale from the first five seconds.*

HOW INVOLVED IS YOUR PROSPECT WHEN YOU MAKE A PRESENTATION?

Tactile (touch, feel) involvement leads to the feeling of ownership. If you want to find out how receptive a prospect is to your product or service, get them involved early and often in the selling process.

Usually it's easier to involve a prospect in a product sale than in a service sale. But if you use your creativity, you'd be amazed at how involved you can get someone.

Involve the customer or prospect in the presentation setup:

- **Ask for help with an easel, slide projector, video machine.**
- **Ask for something – paper, special marker, board eraser.**
- **Ask him to plug things in or help you move something.**
- **Take the offered cup of coffee or soda.**
- **You can even call ahead to request that equipment be ready and in the room for your presentation (markers, projector).**
- **Getting the prospect involved in the set-up gives you additional opportunities for small talk and humor.**

Involve the customer or prospect in the product demonstration: Having your prospects physically involved is the single most important aspect in the presentation process. Let them run the demo, push the button, work the copier, drive the car, hold something, or help you put something together. Even though you know how to do it, you're not going to impress the prospect with a whiz-bang demonstration, you're going to bore him. Get the picture?

Try to let the prospect lead the entire demonstration if possible. The more the prospect does herself (successfully), the more ownership she will take as she gets closer to a decision.

Look and listen for buying signals: big smiles, words of praise, questions, exclamations.

Involve the customer or prospect while explaining a service: Get the prospect to follow along. Read aloud. Play a part in the demonstration. Take a test. Do anything interactive that is fun and creates interest. A 20-minute pitch is not nearly as effective as a 10-minute.

Involve the customer or prospect with ideas and questions: Ask open-ended questions to determine how interested the prospect is…

- **How do you see yourself using …?**
- **If you could use this in your …, when would you …?**
- **How do you see this working in your environment?**
- **Do you see how easy it is to operate?**
- **What are the features you like best?**
- **Let the prospect sell himself – How do you think this will benefit you/your company?**
- **Ask the prospect if she can qualify or afford the product.**

NOTE: When you have finished the demonstration, take things away from the prospect, turn things off, and remove all literature. This eliminates all distractions and keeps you in control of the selling process. If the prospect asks to play with something again or see something again – it's a buying signal. Close on it.

Try to create some involvement that puts a pen in the prospect's hand… This way he's ready when you give him an order form to sign.

Slide show stupidity.
That's not you, is it? Or is it?

In a hotel lobby, I passed by two people involved in a sales presentation. A seller and a buyer. The seller was deeply engrossed in "making the sale." He was intensely looking at his laptop as he methodically flipped through his PowerPoint presentation.

The thing that struck me was that the prospective buyer was not paying the least bit of attention. He was somewhere between staring off in space and completely detached from the presentation.

Noticing this, I went over to the two complete strangers and said to the salesperson, "What are you doing? This guy's not paying any attention to you." Then I turned to the prospect and said, "Are you buying or not?" The prospect, somewhat startled, said, "Yeah, I am." I said, "Great! Finish this transaction right this minute," and walked away grinning.

IT REMINDED ME OF AN OLD SALES JOKE: "Don't buy yet. I'm not finished with my presentation." Now this may be funny to you, but I'll guarantee you that if you have given a PowerPoint presentation you have encountered exactly the same situation. Probably more often than not.

Most sales PowerPoint presentations are somewhere between boring and pathetic. Oh, they can play the message, but in the least engaging way possible. "We do this. We do that. We, we, we-we." Most sales presentations are in terms of the product, the company, and the salesperson. They are not in terms of the only person that matters - the person making the purchase.

The worst part about sales PowerPoint presentations is that they're prepared by someone other than the salesperson – someone who considers himself or herself an expert. Maybe it's the graphics department, maybe it the marketing department – but almost never the sales department. The poor salesperson (that would be you) is forced to use something that is almost anti-sales.

Enough about my rant. Here is the solution.

Here's the list of 16.5 elements to look for, look out for, include, and exclude from you PowerPoint presentation in order to make it engaging and compelling:

1. Don't put more than one point on a slide. SLIDES ARE FREE

2. Add an unexpected, personal, FUNNY (as opposed to humorous) photograph.

3. Make a verbal point and reinforce it with a slide, not the other way around.

4. Don't EVER say, "This one's a little hard to read." SLIDES ARE FREE. Make two of them.

5. Don't have your slides spin around or have sliding type – total waste of time.

6. Don't even think about using stupid clip art that any twelve year old could find. Makes you look like a rank amateur. Use your own clip art, or use none.

7. Count the laughs. At least one per five slides. (If there's at least one laugh every 5 slides, you can count on one other thing: the money.)

8. Use a white background. The fancy ones are distracting and serve no purpose.

9. I put a bug-size logo in the lower right corner of every slide. No idea why, no one has ever said anything to me, but I figure if it's good enough for MTV, I'll do it too.

10. Use the typeface IMPACT. Set the master screen for 44pt and shadow the type.

11. Emphasize words by blowing them up a few point sizes. Make them a different color. I use red.

12. If you're laboring over one slide that you are trying to "make work," delete it. It was probably a weak point anyway.

13. Use slides that tell a story, rather than relate a fact. Stories are the most powerful part of the sale. Here's the rule – facts and figures are forgotten, stories are retold.

14. Are your slides descriptive or engaging? There are two kinds of slides: engaging and disengaging. Review each slide and ask yourself, "How engaging is this slide?" If it's not engaging, why are you using it?

15. Are your slides asking questions, or making statements? Questions will promote conversation and engage. Statements (in general) are unproven, unsubstantiated claims.

16. How many of the claims you make in your sales presentation, whether PowerPoint or verbally, are backed up with proof? Which brings me to my final point.

16.5 Incorporate video testimonial clips throughout your slide presentation to back up, substantiate, and prove that your claims are real, transferable, and acceptable to the customer.

By now you're probably totally disheartened about your PowerPoint presentation. I've exposed it for the un-powerful thing that it is. But take heart. Your competition's sales slide presentation is equally pathetic. Here is the secret solution: Convert the time you're currently wasting watching television re-runs in the evening and develop your own PowerPoint presentation that is 100% in terms of the customer's needs and desires, one that engages the prospective customer by asking questions and promoting dialogue, one that uses a little humor to keep the sales presentation alive, and one that supports every fact and claim with testimonials.

And oh, by the way, there's one question that you better make certain appears towards the end of your PowerPoint presentation. A question that, in one way or another, asks for the sale.

"A live orchestra, costumes, scenery, fireworks, jugglers, elephants, the Rockettes? Can't you just use PowerPoint like everyone else?"

THE SALES BIBLE

The Book of Objections

I object!

The sale starts when the customer says *no*.

If you can turn *no* into *yes*, you make the sale. Simple.

A sale is always made. Either you sell the prospect on *yes*, or he sells you on *no*.

You will hear the word *no* more than 116,000 times in your life.

Your challenge as a salesperson is to change 500 of those *no's* to YES! It will change your life and your bank account.

Don't take *no* for an answer.

Overrule objections.

Here's how…

5.1

Objections, Closing, and
Follow-up. Getting to YES!

Will the real objection please stand up!

The customer says, "I object!" Or does he? Is it the true objection, a stall, or a lie? Euphemistically called *objection* or *concern*, it's actually the real reason a prospect won't buy now. What the prospect or customer is really saying is, "You haven't sold me yet." The prospect is actually requesting more information or more reassurance.

THERE ARE VERY FEW ACTUAL OBJECTIONS. MOST ARE JUST STALLS. This is further complicated by the fact that buyers will often hide the true objection. Why? They don't want to hurt your feelings, they are embarrassed, or they are afraid to tell the truth. A white lie is so much easier, more convenient, and less bloody than actually having to tell the truth, so they just say something to get rid of you.

These are the Top 10 stalls/white lies spoken by a prospect or customer:

1. I want to think about it.
2. We've spent our budget.
3. I have to talk it over with my partner (wife, cat, mistress, broker, lawyer, accountant, shrink).
4. I need to sleep on it.
5. I never purchase on impulse – I always give it time to sink in.
6. I'm not ready to buy yet.
7. Get back to me in 90 days. We'll be ready by then.
8. Quality is not important to me.
9. Business is slow right now.
10. Our ad agency handles that.

"We have a satisfactory source," "We need two other bids," "The home office buys everything," and *"Your price is too high,"* are also classic objections, but I didn't want to ruin the *Top 10* thing.

So, what is a true objection? Most true objections are never stated. 90% of the time when the prospect says, "I want to think it over," or gives you a stalling line, he or she is really saying something else.

Here are the real objections...

- **Doesn't have the money.**
- **Has the money, but is too damn cheap to spend it.**
- **Can't get the credit needed.**
- **Can't decide on his or her own.**
- **Doesn't have authority to spend over budget, or without someone else's financial approval.**
- **Thinks (or knows) he can get a better deal elsewhere.**
- **Has something else in mind, but won't tell you.**
- **Has a friend, connection, or satisfactory relationship in the business.**
- **Does not want to change vendors.**
- **Wants to shop around.**
- **Too busy with other more important things at this time.**
- **Doesn't need (or thinks he doesn't need) your product now.**
- **Thinks (or knows) your price is too high.**
- **Doesn't like or have confidence in your product.**
- **Doesn't like, trust, or have confidence in your company.**
- **Doesn't like, trust, or have confidence in you.**

Finding the *real* objection is the first order of business. It's up there (in the list) someplace. Then (and only then) is successfully overcoming it and making a sale possible.

You can overcome an objection perfectly, but if it isn't the *real* objection, you'll be shaking your head wondering why the sale hasn't been made. When you get an objection, you must determine that it is *true* and the *only one*. Qualifying the objection and overcoming it are of equal importance.

The problem is most salespeople are not able to get to the true objection *and* are not prepared to overcome objections when they occur. Why?

- **They lack the technical (product) knowledge.**
- **They lack the sales tools.**
- **They lack the sales knowledge.**
- **They lack the self-confidence.**
- **They have not prepared in advance (often for the same objection they've heard 10 times before).**
- **Their presentation is lacking.**

Or any combination of the above.

"*The price is too high*" is the classic sales objection. To overcome it, you must find out what the prospect actually means or how high is too high. Half the time you hear it, you're dead.

"I'm here to grant you three wishes: quality, service
and a great price! Eh, make that two wishes!"

Overcoming the true objection.

Real-world objections.
Real-world solutions!

Objections. I love objections. Overcoming them is the true test of a salesperson. The customer isn't exactly saying no; he's just saying not now. *An objection may actually indicate buyer interest.*

Why do objections occur?

1. Because there are doubts or unanswered questions in the mind of the prospect (sometimes created by the salesperson).

2. Because the prospect wants to buy or is interested in buying, but needs clarification, wants a better deal, or must have third-party approval.

3. Because the prospect does not want to buy.

I guarantee you will *get objections if:*

- You have not completely qualified the buyer. (Is he the real decider? Can he really afford it? What is the need and interest level?)

- You have not established need.

- You have not established rapport.

- You have not established credibility.

- You have not established trust.

- You have not found the prospect's hot button.

- Your presentation was weak.

- You have not anticipated objections in your presentation and overcome them before the prospect can raise them.

What's the best way to overcome an objection? Be prepared!

Here are 6.5 steps to identify the true objection and then overcome it:

1. LISTEN CAREFULLY TO THE OBJECTION BEING RAISED. Determine if it is an objection or just a stall. A prospect will often repeat an objection if it's real. Let the prospect talk it out completely. No matter what, agree with the prospect at first. This allows you to tactfully disagree without it starting an argument. If you believe it to be a stall, you must get them to fess up to the real objection or you cannot proceed. If you believe it's a stall, or want clarification, try these lead-in phrases to get to the truth:

- **Don't you really mean ...?**
- **You're telling me _____, but I think you might mean something else.**
- **Usually when customers tell me that, experience has shown me that they really have a price objection. Is that true for you?**

2. QUALIFY IT AS THE ONLY TRUE OBJECTION. Question it. Ask the prospect if it is the only reason he or she won't purchase from your company. Ask if there is any other reason they won't purchase besides the one given.

3. CONFIRM IT AGAIN. Rephrase your question to ask the same thing twice: "In other words, if it wasn't for _____, you'd buy my service. Is that true, Mr. Jones?"

4. QUALIFY THE OBJECTION TO SET UP THE CLOSE. Ask a question in a way that incorporates the solution. "If I'm able to prove the reliability," or "If I'm able to get you extended terms," or "If I'm able to show you the system in a working environment, *would that be enough for you to make a decision?"*

5. ANSWER THE OBJECTION IN A WAY THAT COMPLETELY RESOLVES THE ISSUE. and in a way that the customer ties down to a *yes* answer. Use every tool in your box at this point. If you've got trump cards, play them now (a testimonial video, a comparison chart, a customer you can call on the spot, a special time-related or price-related deal). Forget price – show cost, demonstrate value, list comparisons, and prove benefits. If you cannot answer the prospect in a way that's different or sets you apart from others, you'll never close this (or any) sale. Product knowledge, creativity, sales tools, your belief in yourself, your product and your company, and your ability to communicate, come together in this step. You must combine idea with assurance, sincerity, and conviction to get the prospect to agree with you and mean it.

6. ASK A CLOSING QUESTION, OR COMMUNICATE IN AN ASSUMPTIVE MANNER. Ask a question, the answer to which confirms the sale.

- "If I could … would you" is the classic model for the close.
- "I'm pretty sure we can do this. I have to check one fact with my office. If it's a go on my part, I'm assuming we have a deal," *or* "I could meet with all the decision makers to finalize it."
- Use similar situations when you close. People like to know about others in the same situation.
- Ask, "Why is this/that important to you?" Then use, *"If I could … would you?"*

6.5 CONFIRM THE ANSWER AND THE SALE (IN WRITING WHEN POSSIBLE).
Get the prospect to convert to a customer with a confirming question like:

- When do you want it delivered?
- When is the best starting day to begin?
- Is there a better day to deliver than others?
- Where do you want it delivered?

There are mountains written about closing and overcoming objections. Read every book. Listen to every CD. They all contain ways to overcome objections. And most have usable ideas.

Your job is to apply those ideas to your style and personality.

And the ultimate goal is to make sales in a way that you never have to use them – by establishing relationships and friendships. Sometimes you're precluded from the relationship or friendship, and the ideas are all that's left. That's why you need to know them all.

Free GitBit…**Want the CliffsNotes version of overcoming objections to carry in your wallet?** Go to www.gitomer.com, register if you're a first-time visitor, and enter the words CLIFFS OBJECTIONS in the GitBit box.

"An objection may actually indicate buyer interest."

– *Jeffrey Gitomer*

*If you can anticipate objections,
you can prevent them from occurring.*

Objection Prevention.

"Your price is too high." Rats. Don't you hate when you hear that?

It's the number ONE objection in the world of sales. Why do salespeople continue to listen to it? Beats me.

There are no new objections. You've heard them all before. Can you imagine the prospect saying, "Your price is too high," and you responding, "Really, I've never heard that before." (Actually that response may be better than the one you're using.) Whatever business you're in, there are between 5 and 20 reasons why the customer won't buy now.

Some objections are
stalls – delay tactics or
hesitation by the prospect
to tell the salesperson *no*.
Both objection and stall
are defined by salespeople
in a single word: *frustration*.

Well, here's the way to cure what ails your sales: Prevent objections by discussing them in your presentation *before* the prospect has a chance to voice them. Prevention is the best medicine to cure objections.

Here's how the process works:

• **Identify all possible objections.** Meet with sales reps and customers. Brainstorm objections. Ask them for the top 10 objections they get. They'll flow like water.

• **Write them down.** Make a detailed list of every objection you have identified. Often the same objection is given in a variety of ways.

• **Script objection responses with closing questions for each.** In order to *prevent*, you must *prepare*. It may take some time to complete this task. Do it with your team and perhaps a few customers in the room. Create several scenarios for each objection.

• **Develop sales tools that enhance and support every response.** Items like testimonial letters, testimonial videos, comparison charts, and support documentation can enhance the objection-to-close process. Companies must develop whatever is needed to make the salesperson feel confident, supported, and able to make the sale easier.

• **Rehearse the scripts in role-play.** After the responses are written, schedule several role-play sessions to get familiar with each scripted situation, and try to make it sound natural.

• **Tweak the scripts.** After you role-play, there will be revisions to the scripts. Make them immediately.

• **Try them out on customers.** Go to a problem customer or two. Tell them what you're doing – they'll be flattered that you had the courage, and they'll most often give you truthful responses.

• **Make final revisions based on real-world situations.** The real world always changes a script or approach. Be sure to document revisions every time you make them.

• **Keep the documents in a master notebook.** Give all salespeople a copy. There is an added bonus to this system – when you hire a new salesperson, he or she has a training manual that will provide immediate insight and income.

• **Meet regularly as a group to discuss revisions.** There is always someone inventing the *new* best way possible.

The key is to know the objections that are likely to occur, and script the answers or responses into your regular presentation so that when you come to the end of your pitch, there's nothing to object to.

Here are 7.5 tools and phrases of objection prevention you might consider adding to your scripts and incorporating into your presentation as part of this process:

1. Similar situations – Stories about customers who had the same or similar problem or objection who bought in spite of the objection.

2. Testimonial letters or videos – Some of them can be closers, for example, *"I thought the price was too high, but after a year of lower maintenance cost, I realized the overall cost was actually 20% lower than last year. Thanks for talking me into it."*

3. A story or article about your product or your company – To build support, credibility, and confidence.

4. A comparison chart – Compare the competition apples to apples and use it when the prospect says he wants to check around.

5. Say, "My experience has shown." – One of the most powerful verbal lead-ins to preventing an objection.

6. Say, "I listened to our customers. They had a concern about... Here's what I did..." – To get the prospect to see his potential objection disappear, and how you listen and respond.

7. Say, "I used to believe..., but I've changed and now I..." – As a method of preventing a myth from recurring (reputation for poor service, high price, etc.)

7.5 Prepare yourself – You know the objection is coming. You've heard it before. Be ready with questions, answers, and ideas when it arrives.

If you can overcome an objection in your presentation before the prospect raises it, you are more likely to make a sale.

YOUR REAL WORLD: If you can anticipate objections, you can prevent them from occurring. Sounds simple. It just requires preparation and practice. It takes time, creativity, and focus to make it happen. Please try it. Your reward for superior effort will be superior sales – which lead to a superior wallet.

The sale starts when the customer objects.

Customers won't tell you the real objection first. They'll just stall. But a master salesperson can get through the stall to the real objection.

The following pages are dedicated to overcoming objections – the ones you hear all the time:

- I want to think it over.
- I want to check with two more suppliers.
- Your price is too high.
- I have to talk it over with my partner.
- I'm satisfied with my present supplier.
- We've spent our entire budget for the year.
- Get back to me in six months.

Sometimes these are true objections. Most of the time they're stalls, or worse, untruths.

The key to overcoming objections lies in...

- Your knowledge of selling skills.
- Your knowledge of your product.
- Your knowledge of your prospect.
- The relationship you have with your prospect.
- Your creativity.
- Your attitude.
- Your sincere desire to help your prospect.
- Your persistence.

None of these things has anything to do with price. Some of these things may relate to cost. *All of these things have to do with value.* Each objection in the following pages will focus on a single issue so that you can get as much practical, usable information as possible. My objective is to give you an idea you can use when you make your next sales call.

NOTE: Before you can overcome an objection and make a sale, you have to get down to the true objection.

Here's what to do when the prospect says:

"I want to think about it."

The prospect says, "I want to think about it"? Don't you hate to hear that?

Let's say you're trying to sell Jones Construction a new copier. Jones is interested, but gives you the old line about thinking it over.

"Thinking it over" is a stall, not a true objection.

You can only make the sale if you find out what the true objection(s) is and creatively overcome it.

This will get Mr. Jones off the fence and onto the order pad...

Salesperson: Great! Thinking it over means you're interested. Correct, Mr. Jones?

Jones: Yes, I am.

Salesperson: You're not just saying, "I want to think about it" to get rid of me. Are you? (said in a humorous vein)

Jones: Oh, no, no, no. (laughter)

Salesperson: (seriously) You know, Mr. Jones, this is an important decision. A copier is not just a duplicating device. Every time you send a copy out to a customer, it reflects your company's image. I'm sure you agree with me. Is there anyone else in your company you will be thinking it over with? (Meaning: Is he deciding alone, or are others involved?)

Jones: No, just me.

Salesperson: I know you are an expert at building; your reputation speaks for itself, but I'm an expert in copiers. In my experience in the copier industry over the past 6 years, I've found that most people who think things over develop important questions that they may not have answers for ... since the image of your business is on every copy you make. Why don't we think it over together so that as you develop questions about the copier, I'll be right here to answer them? Fair enough? Now, what was the main thing you wanted to think about? [*At this point you will begin to get the real objection(s).*]

NOTE: If Mr. Jones had said he was going to think it over with others, you must think it over with all parties in the same room, or you're dead.

Here's what to say when the prospect says:

"We spent our entire budget, honest!"

"We spent our entire budget" is one of the best put-offs a prospect can give you. But take heart – **it's only a real objection about half the time**.

- **Sometimes you can find another budget category.**
- **Sometimes you can get a bigger boss to make a variation or exception.**
- **Sometimes the prospect will just use the line to get rid of you.**
- **Sometimes it's the truth – but I'd love to have a dollar for every lie.**

To overcome this objection, you must first find out if the prospect is telling the truth. There are several hidden meaning possibilities: "We spent our whole budget" may actually mean "I can't afford it," *or* "I can buy it elsewhere cheaper (or better)," *or* "I don't want to buy from you (or your company)," *or* "I already have a satisfactory vendor," *or* "I don't want what you've got."

Here are a few ideas to get the prospect off dead center…

- **Mr. Prospect, let me tell you about our deferred payment plan. If you sign for two years now, we can delay payments for six months until your next budget, then simply accelerate payments.**
- **If my service solves your problem, is there any reason why you can't make the necessary changes to be included in your budget?**
- **Who would have the authority to exceed the budget? When can we set up a meeting with them?**

To find out if the prospect truly wants to buy but actually does not have the money in the budget, here's a great method to use:

Salesperson: If the budget wasn't used, would you buy my product?

Prospect: Oh, yes!

Salesperson: When is the next budget meeting?

Prospect: July.

NOTE: You must now ask the following questions and write down the answers.

"What type of proposal do I need to submit?" "Date due?" "Can you get me a sample of a previously submitted proposal?" "Are there others I should submit it to?" "Will you give me a letter of endorsement?" (A letter of endorsement by a manager attached to the budget proposal can be the deciding factor.) "Can I present my proposal in person at the meeting so that any questions can be answered?" (*Any hesitancy on the part of the prospect to answer these questions probably means the budget is not the true or only objection.*)

You might still be able to get a sale or partial sale this year. Begin to ask about the present situation: "Is there anyone else who might be able to rearrange this year's budget to find some money? ... Is there any money left in approved items that is unspent? ... Can we categorize this purchase in another heading that has money left to spend (office equipment, promotion, dues and subscriptions, publicity, advertising)?"

A bit more pushy approach is, "Are you sure you can get it approved?" Prospect says *yes*. You say, "Buy now. I'll bill you now, but it's due after the budget approval."

> "No money in the budget" is among the most difficult objections because you don't know if it's the truth, and if it is, there's serious follow-up that must be done. If you submit a proposal for budget approval, it must be concise, without error, all terms and conditions spelled out, and on time.

You must qualify the fact that the prospect wants your product. Then you can get an endorsement for next year, and potentially some business this year.

Here's what to say when the prospect says:

"I want to check with two more suppliers."

It's frustrating when you have just made a great pitch, you know you have the best product, you have explained every benefit, but the prospect says, "I have to check with two other suppliers." What the heck can you do or say to get the sale today?

The best salespeople are trained to respond to objections and make closes at the appropriate moment. They go to a presentation prepared with every tool that enables them to make the sale now. Below is an idea with a little used but powerful sales tool that can win a sale and impress the prospect with your thoroughness.

SCENARIO: Mr. Jones needs a cellular phone for better and faster business communication, has appointed you, listened to your pitch, but says he wants to look around.

This is probably not his true objection.

Your objective in this situation is to position Mr. Jones in a way that he will buy today or state his true objection. Try this on indecisive Mr. Jones...

Salesperson: You know, Mr. Jones, many of my customers wanted to do the exact same thing before they bought their cell phone from me. I'm sure you want to know you're getting the best phone and the best service for your dollar. Correct?

Jones: Yes, absolutely.

Salesperson: Can you tell me a few of the things you'll be checking (comparing)?

Jones: (Whatever Jonesy says first and second are the real objections – unless he's just trying to get rid of you)

Salesperson: After you have compared these items [name them] with other companies and found ours to be the best, I'm sure you'll buy from us. Correct, Mr. Jones?

Jones: Yes, I will.

OK, it's time to nail Mr. Jones.

Salesperson: Great! Many of our customers want to shop and compare before they buy; but we both know this can take a lot of your valuable time. The reason you're buying the cell phone in the first place is to give you more time. Isn't it? So, to save you the time, we have shopped the competition for you. Here is a chart of our top 20 competitors, their products (show an 11 x 17 chart completely filled in), their services, and their prices for you to review.

Take time to point out how you compare favorably in each area, especially those areas of concern voiced by Mr. Jones.

Now, Mr. Jones, when do you want to sign up for your cell phone plan?

NOTE: Mr. Jones is now pleasantly surprised at how well you did your homework and in shock that he will have to decide now, or else begin to state his true objections. (See *"I want to think about it,"* earlier in this chapter for a list of the true objections you are likely to get.)

A CHART THAT COMPARES YOUR PRODUCTS, SERVICES, AND PRICES WITH THOSE OF YOUR COMPETITION CAN GET YOUR PROSPECT TO BUY NOW INSTEAD OF LOOK AROUND.

A variation of this tactic...
OFFER TO DO THE COMPARISON ON YOUR TIME. Have Mr. Jones tell you what he's going to compare. Tell him you'll file a written comparison, and whoever wins, wins.

Mr. Jones will say, "I don't want you to go to all that trouble." You respond, "Mr. Jones, your business means a lot to me. I don't mind doing this. It'll give me a chance to make sure we're on top of our game. Besides, we've never lost in a competitive comparison."

Now, with the most guts you can muster, say, "Did you want to go ahead and sign up now, or wait until the comparison is over?"

Here's what to do when the prospect says:

"I want to buy, but the price is too high."

Mercedes-Benz is one of the most expensive cars in the world. Some people say, "The price is too high" … the company sells thousands of autos worldwide. Mercedes is one of the wealthiest companies in the world.

"The price is too high" has been a cry from buyers since the open market in Damascus, 2,000 years ago … but they still bought.

"The price is too high" is a classic objection. To overcome it, you must find out what the prospect actually means. Assuming he or she wants to buy now, and the person you're speaking to is the sole decider, there are actually five possible meanings behind this objection…

1. **I CAN'T AFFORD IT.**
2. **I CAN BUY IT ELSEWHERE CHEAPER (OR BETTER).**
3. **I DON'T WANT TO BUY FROM YOU (OR YOUR COMPANY).**
4. **I DON'T SEE, PERCEIVE, UNDERSTAND THE COST OR VALUE OF YOUR PRODUCT OR SERVICE.**
5. **I'M NOT CONVINCED YET.**

About half the time you get a price objection, you will not make the sale. That leaves a 50% opportunity window. Open it.

Here are some probes you can try…

- **Prove affordability:** "What we will do for you costs less in comparison to what it will cost you if you don't hire us and proceed on your present course."
- **Challenge:** "What are you willing to pay?" "What price can you afford?"
- **Get a feel for the difference:** "How much 'too high' is it?"
- **Talk about value and tomorrow:** "Mr. Jones, you're thinking about pennies per day. We're talking about value over a lifetime."

The one that has worked best for me is: "Would you buy it from me now (not today) if the price were lower?" (Assume the prospect says yes.) "You mean other than price, there is no reason we can't do business?"

NOTE: I have double-qualified the prospect on the price objection to determine it is the real, true, and ONLY objection. "If we can figure a way to make it affordable, will you take delivery or begin or order right away?"

If the prospect says yes, then you have to creatively figure out a way to change the terms, offer a discount, offer a future credit of items to enhance value, compare price to cost (over a term), or simply resell at the original price.

The key is to prepare these answers in advance. You know the objection is coming. Why be surprised?

If prospects want your product or service bad enough, they'll figure out a way to afford it. Just because they say the price is too high, doesn't mean they won't buy.

What is actually being said many times is "I want to buy. Show me a way."

Just because a prospect says, "The price is too high," doesn't mean he won't buy today.

Here's what to do when the prospect says:

"I'm satisfied with my present source."

Great, just what you wanted to hear. But don't get discouraged with this one; it's actually pretty easy to get an opening and begin a relationship if you can get the prospect talking. Just because he's satisfied now doesn't mean he'll stay that way.

Realize that what your prospect is saying is that their existing supplier is the best they've been able to find.

You may have a better product, price, availability for delivery, service, training, or warranty. The prospect is only telling you he's satisfied from *his perspective.* He doesn't really know about you or your company yet.

Knowing the reason why the relationship is satisfactory will help you understand how to proceed.

Here are the top 12 reasons your prospect likes the vendor he's currently using...

1. Price or great deal (perceived value).
2. Quality of product/service.
3. Has a special business relationship.
4. Has a personal relationship.
5. Has used this supplier for years.
6. Doesn't know any better – only thinks he's getting a good deal or good service.
7. Vendor "helped me when I needed it."
8. Great (friendly, immediate) service.
9. In stock – immediate delivery.
10. Personalized service/does favors.
11. Told by others, "This is who we buy from."
12. Is lazy, has a vendor, doesn't want to change, isn't spending his own money (not the boss).

Find out which one of these 12 reasons applies to your situation before you start to overcome this objection...or you're wasting your time.

Here's what to do when the prospect says:

"I have to talk this over with my…"
Uh oh!

When you hear the words "I have to talk this over with…," you realize you've done something very wrong. You didn't qualify the prospect very well, did you? OK. What do you do now?

When others need to approve the deal, besides qualifying the buyer better, you must take four action steps…

1. **Get the prospect's personal approval.**
2. **Get on the prospect's team.**
3. **Arrange a meeting with all deciders.**
4. **Make your entire presentation again.**

If you think you can get around these steps, think again. It's obvious you're looking for shortcuts or you would have properly qualified the buyer. If you would have just asked, "Is there anyone else you work with on decisions like these?" this whole mess wouldn't be taking place. Would it?

Back to the reality of the four steps…

1. GET THE PROSPECT'S PERSONAL APPROVAL. "Mr. Jones, if it was just you and you didn't need to confer with anyone else, would you buy it?" (The prospect will almost always say yes.) I ask, "Does this mean you'll recommend our product to the others?"

Now I go through a checklist that seems a little redundant, but I want to uncover any areas of doubt, so I ask…

- **Is the price OK?**   • **Is the product OK?**
- **Is the service OK?**   • **Is the company OK?**
- **Am I OK?**   • **What doubts do you have?**
- **Do you like it well enough to own it?**

NOTE: *Revise these questions to suit what you sell. Revise them in a more personalized way. The objective is to nail down absolute approval.* Get the prospect to endorse you and your product to the others, but don't let him (or anyone) make your pitch for you.

2. GET ON THE PROSPECT'S TEAM. Begin to talk in terms of "we," "us," and "the team." By getting on the prospect's team, you can get the prospect on your side of the sale.

- "What do WE have to do?"
- "When can WE get them together?"
- "When does the team meet next? It's important that I am present because I'm sure they'll have questions that they will want answers to."
- "What can I do to be a member of the team?"
- "Tell me a little bit about the others." (Write down every characteristic.) Try to get the personality traits of the other deciders.

3. ARRANGE A MEETING WITH ALL DECIDERS. Do it any way you have to. Leave several alternative *open times* from your date book. Use the alternatives as a reason to get back and solidify your meeting with the decision-making group.

4. MAKE YOUR ENTIRE PRESENTATION AGAIN. You only have to do this if you want to make the sale. Otherwise just leave it to the prospect. He thinks he can handle it and will try his best to convince you of that.

The best way for you to make this (or any) sale is to be in control of the situation. If you make the mistake of letting your prospect become a salesperson on your behalf (goes to the partner instead of you), you will lose. Every time.

An alternative method...

Ask the prospect if he's sure the partner (wife, boss) will want to do the deal. If the prospect says, "Yes, I'm sure," you say, "Great! Why not just approve the purchase now [sign the contract], and get their approval? If you call me tomorrow and tell me no, I'll tear up the contract. Fair enough?"

You can avoid and prevent this objection with three words...

Qualify
the buyer!

Here's what to do when the prospect says:

"*Call me back in 6 months.*"

Is it just a polite way of saying no? *Are you willing (do you have the guts) to bottom-line the prospect?*

Pat me on the head and tell me to go away. That's the real meaning of *"Call me in 6 months"* (or any nebulous "get back to me" after some period of time). The prospect is really saying no! To overcome this stall, you must find out what true obstacles are in the way.

Does the buyer really want your product? Is there someone else? Is your price too high? Can the prospect afford what you're selling?

Fact is, if the prospect says "Call me in 6 months," you haven't found the true reason for the stall (and may not want to know). The real reasons for this objection are:

1. You have not established enough rapport.
2. You have not established enough buyer confidence.
3. You have not established enough need.
4. You have not established enough value.
5. You have not established enough trust.
6. You have not established enough desire.
6.5 You have not established a sense of urgency to buy today.

You've done all that? The prospect is telling you the truth? Baloney. If you are looking for some truth in rejection, try looking a bit deeper. The real reason might be one of these:

- The prospect isn't the true decider.
- The prospect doesn't have the money.
- The prospect doesn't like your company.
- The prospect doesn't like your product.
- The prospect thinks your price is too high.
- The prospect has a friend or relationship established to buy or get your product or service in some other (more beneficial) way.
- The prospect doesn't like you.

Here are some questions to try:

- What will be different in 6 months?

- Is there a particular reason you prefer that I get back to you in 6 months?

- What is preventing you from taking action today?

BIG QUESTION: Are you willing (do you have the guts) to bottom-line the buyer? Do you have the courage to ask him, "Are you really saying NO?"

If you want to begin the process to overcoming this objection (stall) and finding out where the sale is, do any one or combination of the following:

- Ask the prospect, "Do you see yourself buying in 6 months?"

- Find out who else is involved in the decision by asking, "How will the decision be made?"

- Ask the prospect, "Could you purchase now and pay in 6 months?"

- Show that by purchasing now the prospect will save/earn back some or all of the purchase price in 6 months.

- Show how a delay can cost more than purchasing now.

- Ask if he has looked at the cost of delay.

- Show how the advantage of purchasing now outweighs the hidden expense of waiting.

- Show the difference between spend (cash outlay) and cost (total value of the sale).

BIG ANSWER: Wherever the answer lies (and often the prospect does just that), one fact is clear: A 6-month, 6-week, or 6-day stall is not the fault of the prospect. You have not uncovered the true desire, need, or objection.

It's not an issue
of blame – it is an
issue of responsibility.
Yours.

THE SALES BIBLE

Part 5
Objections, Closing, and
Follow-up. Getting to YES!

The Book of Closing

Objections, Closing and Follow-up. Getting to YES!

Closing...

That was your first close. And sometimes it worked.

The sale belongs to the closer...
It pays (big commissions) to master the science of the close.

All your work, all your preparation, comes down to one final question.

The close is a delicate balance between your words and actions and the prospect's thoughts and perceptions.

Here's how to ask for the sale and get it!

5.2

*Any question asked by the prospect
must be considered a buying signal.*

What are the 19.5 early warning signals that the prospect is ready to buy?

QUESTION: When is the prospect ready to buy?

ANSWER: He'll tell you if you just pay attention.

The links between the presentation and the close are buying signals. Recognizing signals to buy is the first step toward a close in the science of selling. Listen to the buyer. He or she will give you signals.

When you're giving your presentation, the buyer will gesture, question, play with your product, or in some way communicate that he is inclined to purchase. As a professional salesperson, your job is to recognize the buying signal and convert it into a sale.

Here are 19.5 signals (questions) to look for:

1. Questions about availability or time. *Are these in stock? How often do you receive new shipments?*

2. Questions about delivery. *How soon can someone be here? How much notice do I have to give you?*

3. Specific questions about rates, price, or statements about affordability. *How much does this model cost? What is the price of this training program? I don't know if I can afford that model.*

4. Any questions or statements about money. *How much money would I have to put down to get this?*

5. Positive questions about your business. *How long have you been with the company? How long has your company been in business?*

6. Wanting something repeated. *What was that you said before about financing?*

7. Statements about problems with previous vendors. *Our old vendor gave us poor service. How quickly do you respond to a service call?*

8. Questions about features and options – what your product or service does. *Is the sorter standard or optional?*

9. Questions about quality. *How many copies per month is the machine rated for?*

10. Questions about guarantee or warranty. *How long is this under warranty?*

11. Questions about qualifications – your's or the company's. *Can all of your people answer questions over the phone?*

12. Specific positive questions about the company. *What other products do you carry?*

13. Specific product/service questions. *How does the manual feed operate? Do you select the person or do I?*

14. Specific statements about ownership of your product or service. *Would you provide paper each month automatically? Will you come by each month to pick up my accounting? Suppose I like her and want her to work for me full-time?*

15. Questions to confirm unstated decisions or seeking support. *Is this the best way for me to go?*

16. Wanting to see a sample or demo again. *Could I see the fabric samples again?*

17. Asking about other satisfied customers. *Who are some of your current or best customers?*

18. Asking for a reference. *Could I contact someone you have done training for in the past? Do you have a list of references?*

19. Buying noises. *I didn't know that. Oh really. That's interesting. That's in line with what we've been doing.*

19.5 Your ability to convert the signal into a sale. *Every one of these buying signals (questions) can be turned into a closing question that will lead to a faster sale – if you do it right.*

How do you answer these questions? Good question! A buying signal. I'll tell you in the next chapter.

"Recognizing buying signals is critical to your success as a salesperson. You will go past the sale if you fail to recognize them. And many do."

— *Jeffrey Gitomer*

*If you answer a prospect's question with
yes or no, you may be going past
the sale without making it.*

When you answer a prospect's question, avoid two words – Yes and No.

When a prospect asks me a yes or no question, *I never answer yes or no.*
When a prospect asks me any question, I try to answer in the form of a
question – or ask a question at the end of my answer. This establishes two
of the central objectives in selling:

1. **I'm in control of the presentation.**
2. **My ability to close the sale has increased.**

THINK ABOUT IT FOR A MOMENT. When a prospect asks you a question, it is
often a buying signal. How do *you* answer their question? As a salesperson,
your highest skills are called upon when a prospect asks a question or
shows an interest in buying. Your first inclination is to answer the question
in the affirmative, if you know it to be true. *For example:*

- **"Do you have this model?"** *Yes.*
- **"Does it come in green?"** *Yes.*
- **"Can you deliver on Tuesday?"** *Yes.*
- **"Are these in stock?"** *Yes.*

All of the above yes answers are not only wrong, they are answers that
prolong the sale unnecessarily.

You are also inclined to answer the prospect in a straightforward manner.
For example:

- **"What is your delivery lead time?"** *Usually 2 weeks.*
- **"How much notice do I have to give you?"** *24 hours.*
- **"When will the new model be out?"** *January 30th.*

These answers are also wrong. Very wrong.

THE RULE IS: Use the prospect's question to confirm the sale. In other words, after you get the prospect's signal, form a response question that implies the answer and confirms that the prospect wants to buy what you're selling.

It's not as complicated as I just made it sound.

Here are some examples of confirming questions:
- **"Do you have this model?"** *Is this the model you want?* If the prospect says *yes*, all I have to do now is find out when he wants delivery, and I'm finished.
- **"Does it come in green?"** *Would you like it in green?*
- **"Can you deliver on Tuesday?"** *Is Tuesday the day you need it delivered?*
- **"Are these in stock?"** *Do you need immediate delivery?*
- **"What is your delivery lead time?"** *How soon do you need delivery?*
- **"How much notice do I have to give you?"** *How much notice do you usually have?*
- **"How soon can someone be here?"** *How soon do you need someone here?*

You can also answer directly and still pose a closing question immediately thereafter. *For example:*
- **"When will the new model be out?"** *January 30. But we have special incentives to take the copier now. Let's compare which will be the best way for you to go. Fair enough?*
- **"Do you have references?"** *Here is the list. If our references are satisfactory, when would we be able to get our first assignment?*

Here's the magic process:
1. **Recognizing a buying signal is the sales discipline.**
2. **Being able to construct a response question (much more difficult) requires creativity and practice.**
2.5 **Delivering the response soft and smooth is the mark of the master professional salesperson. And usually the one who makes the sale.**

How to ask a closing question.

Thousands of pages have been written on closing the sale. You can have the best presentation in the world, you can be an expert in your product or your field of endeavor, but if you don't know how to close the sale, dining out for you will probably mean a drive-thru window.

The experts (J. Douglas Edwards, Zig Ziglar, Tom Hopkins, Earl Nightingale, etc.) define closing as: *Asking a question, the answer to which confirms the sale.* After you ask this all-important question, it is critical that you follow the oldest rule of selling: *After you ask a closing question, SHUT UP! The next person who speaks loses.*

THERE ARE THOUSANDS OF WAYS TO ASK FOR THE SALE: But you can set the tone for closing by telling the prospect what you want (the purpose or objective of your meeting) when you walk in the door. *Then, ask for the sale as soon as you hear the first buying signal.* An important guideline in asking for the sale is to try to eliminate *no* as a possible response to your question. You may not get the coveted *yes* as a result of eliminating the word *no*, but you will get dialogue or objections that will eventually lead to a *yes*.

Formulate your closing question in a way that responds to the prospect's main need or desire.

HERE ARE SOME EXAMPLES: "Mr. Jones, would you like these t-shirts in light or dark colors?" or "How many shirts do you want in the darker color you said you liked?" or "Would you like delivery before or after the first of next month?" or "When do you want these delivered?" or "Are you paying by check or credit card?"

These are examples of using time, choice, or preference methods – simple ideas that eliminate *no* as a response.

Let the buyer decide, but don't give him or her *no* as one of the choices.

Other closing questions offer a possible *no* response. Before you ask this type of closing question, be sure you have confirmed the prospect's interest and he has given you concrete buying signals.

FOR EXAMPLE: You're trying to sell Mr. Jones a fax machine. Jones says he needs a machine by Tuesday, but has not yet said he is buying from you. You ask, "Would you like me to deliver your new fax machine Monday evening?" *That is a solid closing question.* You have given the prospect the option of saying no, but it is unlikely he'll use it. (Even if Jones says *no*, ask: "When *would be* the most convenient time to make delivery?")

The key is to ask for the sale in a sincere, friendly manner. Don't push or use high pressure. If you just stop talking after you ask the closing question, the tension in the air mounts real fast.

A minute seems like an hour when the room is silent.

Self-confidence is important. The buyer will buy if you believe he will. Most salespeople don't ask for the sale because they're afraid of rejection, uncomfortable about the money, or not sharp enough to recognize the buying signals of a customer. I'm glad none of those apply to you.

The oldest rule of sales still holds true…

When you ask a question, the answer to which confirms the sale…

Shut up!

In my experience I have found the biggest flaw in failing to secure the order is the salesperson's inability to know when and how to ask for it.

The sale belongs to the closer.
People love to be closed.

*The sale is more likely to be made
if the prospect can take ownership before
she actually commits to the sale.*

The Puppy Dog Close.

How can you adapt its power to your sales process?

The easiest way to sell a puppy is to give it to the prospective owner (and the kids) overnight to "see how they like it." Then try to get the puppy back from the kids the next morning! Thus the name "Puppy Dog Close." It's an incredibly powerful sales tool that is used (with variation) by salespeople around the world.

Think about it for a moment…

- **Test drive the car.**
- **30-day free trial membership.**
- **Try this in your home for 7 days.**
- **First issue of the magazine is free.**
- **2-day demo of our copier in your office.**

All these are forms of the Puppy Dog Close.

You're telling the prospect your product is great – but they may not know it until they touch it, try it, take it home, or use it. If you can get the prospect to touch and try your product, you're more likely to get him to buy it.

It's ownership before the sale. It breaks down resistance to the point of acceptance.

Obviously not all businesses can use the Puppy Dog Close, but more and more corporate sales strategies call for trying to get the product into the hands of the buyer for a test or trial as part of the selling process.

When you try on a new suit or dress, before you make the purchase, you see yourself owning it…The fit, the feel, the look, and the salesperson chortling how good it looks, are often more influential than the price. You can almost envision yourself at the office or trade show in your new clothing. Then you say, "OK, I'll take it."

If you doubt the power of this close, go to a pet store and ask if you can have a puppy overnight for evaluation. You might want to take your checkbook along, just in case.

How old is the Puppy Dog Close? God gave Moses the 10 Commandment Tablets. "Try them," he said. Pretty strong close. Still working. After 5,000 years, he still has billions of customers.

"You mean I have to sell these?"

"If you chase the world, it runs from you.
If you run from the world, it chases you."
— Hari Dass

Let the dog chase you

When I was 16, I decided to get a puppy. Early one morning the puppy got away. She ran for blocks through the neighborhood as I chased her fruitlessly. I was panicked. Surely the dog would get hit by a car. I ran home as fast as I could to awaken my dad to get in the car and find my dog. Dad reluctantly began to get out of bed. I spun to race to the car – and tripped over the dog.

The sales moral of the story is: Let the prospect chase you. Sometimes you're better off baiting or challenging the prospect. Often you are so eager to sell, you don't give the prospect enough room to buy.

There are variations of this technique that are from the old school of selling but are still worth looking at…

THE NEGATIVE SALE. (Take it away if the buyer shows interest) It has been touted through the years as the most powerful selling device. When motel franchises were first sold in the 1950s, a salesman would come into town, visit a local bank, and say there were "only" 10 shares in this new motel at $50,000 per share. He would ask the banker for leads – and get them. He would make group presentations that started out, "I believe all the shares are spoken for, but I'll go through my presentation, take your application, and if I get a cancellation, I'll give you a call." I was with my friend's dad that day. He eagerly filled out the application. To his amazement, he was called – someone had canceled. We found out later everyone was called.

Good tactic? Well, it worked. Ethical? You decide.

THE "CAN YOU QUALIFY?" SALE. Rather than pushing the prospect to buy, you challenge him to qualify (have the money, get the credit) for purchase.

Often used in door-to-door sales, or big items requiring credit, like cars and homes. You can laugh at it, but it still is the backbone of the sales efforts of many national companies.

How soon do you close a sale?
As soon as you walk in the door!

Eat dessert first!

You're at one of those banquets where they put out the salad and dessert before anyone arrives. So, when I sit down, I immediately eat the dessert. People are anywhere from surprised to shocked. If they make a comment, I ask if they're going to eat theirs. If they say no, I ask them to pass it over.

If someone gives me a choice of apple pie and ice cream or lima beans, I'm not an idiot. Dessert is to eating as closing is to selling. It's the best part. Tradition says do it last – I say do it first.

I begin to close the sale within 10 seconds of entering a prospect's office. I state my objective for the meeting, and I tell him or her what I would like to do.

I tell them my three strategies of business:
- **I'm here to help.**
- **I seek to establish a long-term relationship.**
- **I'm going to have fun.**

Stating your objective and philosophy at the outset puts the prospect at ease. It gets the meeting off to a great start. It establishes credibility and respect. And it clears the way for meaningful information exchange and rapport building.

Tell the prospect what you want when you walk in the door. Then, ask for the sale as soon as you hear the first buying signal.

You were raised to think in patterns set by others. To be as successful as you want to be, it may take getting out of those traditional patterns. Most people don't get out of their comfort zone. Most people don't attain the level of success they set out to achieve. I wonder if there's any correlation between those two statements?

DON'T SAVE ROOM FOR DESSERT. EAT IT FIRST! It's a sweet way to close.

Understand how your product is used
so that you can understand
how to sell it most effectively.

The most powerful close in the world is not a close.
The Understanding Close

Product knowledge is useless until you know how your product is used on the job in a way that the customer can benefit from and profit from. On the surface this seems simple, but I challenge you as to how far you have gone to understand how your customers actually use your product or service on a real-world, day-to-day basis. How do they use it in their work environment?

In most cases, the end user is not the purchaser. The person who buys the copier or computer is seldom the person who runs it every day. The end user is the person who will lead you to important sales information.

It's easy to find out. Go visit your customers. Watch, ask, and listen.

- Go watch your product being used.
- Ask questions about their likes and dislikes.
- Ask what they like best.
- Ask what they like least.
- Ask what they would change and how they would change it.
- Ask about service they've received after the sale.
- Observe the operations made by everyone connected.
- Ask if they would buy it again.
- Ask if they would recommend it to a business associate.
- Write down or record everything they say!

Seeing your product in action and questioning its use puts a new (and powerful) perspective on how you sell it:

- It's customer insight at its highest level.
- It's product knowledge that no factory training can provide.
- It's the best (and least-used) opportunity to gain knowledge about a customer's real needs.
- It's a chance to see the benefits of your product in action.

When your visit is over...

- Document it.
- Thank your customers for their time.
- Report what changed as a result of it.
- Make recommendations.

Try to measure the value of these five benefits...

1. You've built incredible rapport.
2. You've taken giant relationship steps.
3. Competition will have a tougher time getting in the door.
4. You've gained indispensable knowledge that will lead you to more sales.
5. Your customer now sees you as a consultant rather than a salesman.

ON A SALES CALL: Discuss using the product in the customer's work environment and have a hands-on basis for your expertise. Ask questions that get the prospect talking about use after purchase. "If you purchased, how would you use this differently than the one you have now?"

And if you do it right, it's not only a learning opportunity. It's a selling opportunity.

THE SALES BIBLE

Part 5
Objections, Closing, and
Follow-up. Getting to YES!

The
Book of
Persistence

Blood, Sweat, & Commissions

Persistence...

I could retitle this
The Book of Pest Control.
How to follow-up without
bugging the client.

Persistence
(with the right attitude)
is the key to success.

If you believe in your
product, if you believe in
yourself, then you march to
success.

Obstacles can't stop you.
Problems can't stop you.
Most important of all, other
people can't stop you.

Only you can stop you.

Persistence is your desire
to succeed combined with
your creative presence.

Your persistence must be as
relentless as the tides.

Roll on...

5.3

Sales tools are a vital part of the follow up process.

Your ability to create follow up selling tools can significantly enhance your image with the prospect and make the sale more often.

Defined as an aid or prop in the selling process, sales tools can be a tremendous boost to productivity, especially if several follow ups are needed to make the sale.

There are everyday tools like the phone, email, letters, brochures, and literature, but the extraordinary salesperson creates out-of-the-ordinary tools to entice the prospect to buy now and to choose his or her product over the competition.

Review the tools listed below and see if they might be effective in your sales game plan:

• **Personal note (imprinted with your company name and logo, greeting card size) ... handwritten.** Better and more effective than the common business letter. Gives the prospect the feeling that you care.

• **A package of letters from loyal customers.** No salesperson is more persuasive than third-party endorsements.

• **A third-party mutual friend endorsement.** An incredibly powerful tool. Your friend is far more influential than you.

• **Support articles.** Like a copy of a favorable article recently printed that can give you an additional reason to mail and call. It doesn't have to be about your business. It's better if it's about his business or best if it's about his personal interests.

• **Video supporting your product/service.** Prepared by you or your supplier; if a picture is worth 1,000 words, a video is worth 1,000,000.

• **Meet at a networking event (lead club, chamber function, etc.).** Business/ social engagements are the heart of business life.

• **An invitation to your facility.** Building the business relationship by showing yours with pride. A welcome sign for the visitor, and happy, enthusiastic greetings by all members of your team. Make the tour memorable. Serve great food. Ask yourself: Will the prospect go back to his office and talk about this visit? If not, change it so he will.

• **Ad specialty.** Small, useful (Post-it Note pad, coffee mug, T-shirt), or unusual item that will be used, seen, or talked about.

• **Lunch appointment.** Spending a few extra dollars can often lead to the sale. It will also get the personal information that leads to a relationship.

• **After-work meeting.** Meeting the prospect after hours can be more relaxed and informative. Get to know and like your prospect. People will buy from their friends first.

• **Tickets.** Sporting events, cultural events, and seminar tickets are appreciated and can help build a relationship. (Go with the customer.)

• **Telephone.** The second most powerful weapon in selling (live visits being the first). Calls can set up meetings, give information, and close the deal; but calls can get redundant, and many times don't get returned. It's also hard to get a signed contract over the phone, and checks don't squeeze through the little holes very well. Use the phone with respect. Stay in control at all times. Have a purpose for calling. NEVER end the call without having set the next meeting or contact.

"If you convert the numbers from Celsius to Fahrenheit,
adjust for inflation, score on a curve, and factor dog years
into the equation, my sales are up 850 percent this quarter!"

*Somewhere between diapers and getting
our business card printed, we forget how
tenacious we need to be to make that sale.*

You've been selling
since you were a kid!

*I would like to acknowledge Joe Bonura, of Bonura Training Systems,
whose excellent seminar provided the inspiration for this story.*

How many *no*'s are you willing to take before you give up the sale?
Remember when you were seven years old, in line with your mother at
the supermarket, and asked, "Mom, can I have this candy bar?" *That was a
closing question if there ever was one.*

"No," she replies. You, the master salesman, ignore the first *no* and
respond, "Please, can I have the candy bar?" Mom is a bit put off by now;
with her mind preoccupied with the grocery tab, she says, "I said NO!" *No*
number two is now safely out of the way, and you respond, "Aw, come on,
PLEASE!"

Now the momma prospect is emphatic. "Absolutely NO," she thunders *no*
number three. (Sometimes she will actually spell it out: N-O.) *No* number
three is now out of the way. Time to move in for the kill. Let's try to find
out what the objection is here. "Why can't I have a candy bar, Mom?" This
is a classic example of a direct question going straight at the real reason
for the first three *no*'s. How did you learn these sales skills so early in life?

"Because it'll spoil your dinner," she responds, true to form. Now is your
big chance. Overcome this objection (the fourth put-off), and it's in the
bag (the grocery bag, that is). "No it won't, Mom. I promise to eat it after
dinner," you reply in your most sincere tone.

She's on the ropes now, about to cave in, but being the true sales-reluctant
prospect, she isn't going to just cave in. "Well, I don't know," she weakly
states the fifth negative response. You see your opening and immediately

bellow, "PLEASE!" in that endearing kid mixture of song and whine. "OK," she says. "But don't you dare eat it until *after* dinner." (She has to get out of the loss gracefully, so she emphasizes the caveat "after dinner" to save face to the cashier, who is grinning.)

VICTORY! You made the sale, and it only took five *no*'s to get it. You were prepared to go at least 10. Possibly risk a hit or two on the butt, and in some cases actually throw a fit in public. Think about that for a second. When you were seven, you were willing to risk public embarrassment, corporal punishment, and verbal abuse to make the sale.

Somewhere between diapers and getting your business card printed, you forgot how tenacious you need to be to make that sale.

If you're looking for the best examples of how to overcome the obstacles and objections to sales, just sit back and reminisce. The candy bar, the first date, staying out after curfew, getting the keys to the car, getting a raise in allowance, or getting off punishment to go to the dance – all sales. All were full of *no*'s and objections. But did you hang in there against all odds? Were you willing to risk? Willing to take a beating? Did you eventually make the sale?

I'll bet your closing ratio as a kid was better than 90%.

How much money would you be making if your closing ratio were that high today? Forget candy bars – you'd have enough cash to buy the entire grocery store.

On average it takes seven impressions, exposures, no's, or objections to get the sale. What's the secret to getting to the seventh no? Persistence.

The big question is
Do you leave a message?
The big answer is
It depends!

Oh, no! Not voicemail!

Press 1 … If you want to leave a message.

Press 2 … If you don't think your call will ever be returned.

Press 3 … If you've already left three messages, haven't had your call returned, and want to send a bolt of lightning directly through the phone to strike the butt of the person who won't return your call.

Press 4 … If you want to shoot the person who installed this voicemail.

Voicemail can be the scourge of the salesperson, but it doesn't have to be.

It's a tool used to establish contact. It is not used to make a sale.
Your objective is to leave a message that will elicit a return call.

HERE'S AN ALTERNATIVE: Ignore voicemail and use your resourcefulness to get in direct contact with your prospect.

Here are four guidelines that define the sales perspective of voicemail:

1. **It's a game – play to win.**

2. **It's here to stay – know how to get around it.**

3. **Know how to leave a message that will get a response.**

4. **Be resourceful. Be creative. Be memorable.**

Here are some ideas for getting around voicemail and getting directly to the prospect:

- **Press "0" to get an operator or secretary.**
  Ask if the prospect can be paged.
- **Tell the operator you don't want voicemail and ask how you can reach your prospect live.**
- **Tell an administrative person you got lost in the voicemail options, you're not a college graduate, and can they please help you.** If you *nicely* act exasperated, you can get someplace – especially at the CEO executive administrative level.
- **Find the administrative person and get the prospect's schedule of normal arrival and departure.**
- **Get someone else to book a tentative appointment.**
- **Call before the gatekeeper arrives**
  (7:45 to 8:30 A.M.).
- **Call after the gatekeeper leaves**
  (5:15 to 6:30 P.M.).
- **Call the sales department** – they'll tell you everything if they think you can help. Plus they're more fun to deal with than administrative types.
- **In a larger company, call the publicity or public relations department** – it's their job to give out information.
- **Find a champion or comrade** – someone within the company who likes you or believes in what you do.

For years I struggled with "should you leave a message or not." I finally arrived at what I believe to be the best answer. Always leave a message. Even if it's just your name and your phone number, there's no reason not to leave a message. While I realize that voicemail can be frustrating, you have to look at it as an opportunity to make a connection and the challenge of being creative in order to get your call returned. If you don't leave a message, it's because you have nothing of value to say.

NOTE WELL: If you have no value message, and you DO get through, it's likely that the customer will just hang up anyway. Your challenge is to beat voicemail by using the one sales tool you always carry with you – your brain.

"Leave a message and I'll be glad to return your call." Not!

"Press 1 if you'd like to leave a message. I'll be glad to return your call as soon as I can." Right. And Santa will bring you a pony if you're a good little boy.

"Press 2 if you're selling something I don't want." That's a lot closer to the truth.

Why won't they call you back? When you get someone's voicemail and decide to leave a message, what steps can you take to ensure that your call will be returned? Lots.

If you leave a message, here is a collection of ideas that have gotten calls returned:

• **First name and number only (in a very businesslike manner).** It seems that calls are returned in inverse proportion to the amount of information left.

• **Be funny.** Clean wit will get response.

• **Be indirect.** "I was going to mail you important information and I wanted to confirm your address."

• **Offer fun.** "I have two extra tickets to the Eagles game and I thought you might be interested." Here's the sure shot: "Please call me if you can't go so that I'm able to give the tickets to someone else."

• **Remind the prospect where you met if it was a positive first meeting.**

• **Dangle the carrot.** Leave just enough information to entice.

• **Ask a provocative or thought-provoking question.**

NOTE: There is never a reason to give your sales pitch on voicemail. No one is there to say yes. Your objective is to make contact. Your objective is to provide enough information to create positive response.

AN ALL-TIME CLASSIC IDEA…was offered by Thomas J. Elijah III, of Elijah & Co. Real Estate, at a SalesMasters™ meeting. Thomas said, "Leave a partial message that includes your name and phone number, then pretend to get cut off in midsentence as you're getting to the important part of the message. Cut it off in midword. It works like a charm because the prospect can't stand not knowing the rest of the information or thinks his voicemail is broken."

Here are a few examples of the Elijah Method: Leave your name and number, then deliver half a sentence to peak interest:

- **Your name came up in an important conversation today with Hugh…**
- **They were talking about you and said…**
- **I have a deal that could deliver you a hundred thou…**
- **I'm interested in your…**
- **I have your…**
- **I found your…**
- **I have information about your…**
- **Your competition said…**
- **I'm calling about your inheritance…**
- **Are you the [person's full name] who…**
- **We wanted to be sure you got your share of…**
- **I'm calling about the money you left at…**
- **Hello. I'm calling for Ed Mc…**

I had to call Elijah recently to get some information. I tried his idea on him, cutting off my message in midsentence. I said, "I'm going to quote you in my column this week and I need…" He called me back in under three minutes, laughing hysterically. This idea could revolutionize message leaving. I've been using it ever since, and it works. *Be careful about how far you go on the humor with someone you don't know.*

If you're making several calls, make sure you document your messages so that you can be on top of it immediately if/when your call is returned. There's nothing worse (or more stupid) than getting a returned call and having no idea who it's from. Voice messaging companies say that voicemail helps companies route messages faster, and the recording system offered by voice messaging reduces errors and allows complete messages to be left. True, but many of the people who have voicemail (especially the ones you're trying to reach) use it as a dodge.

If you're thinking about buying voicemail, don't just look at convenience. Before you make a commitment to a specific system, consider the impact on your customers.

Will they be better served? Will you maintain friendly, human service in spite of the voice-mail system?

Don't confuse voicemail with automatic attendant systems. Automatic attendant, where the computer actually answers the phone, is the single worst business invention ever.

Here is the most customer-friendly type of voice-mail system to use:

1. **Human answers.**

2. **Human determines if the person you're calling is in by ringing their phone and monitoring the response.**

3. **If not in, human returns and says, "Mr. Jones is not in. Would you like me to help you personally, take your message personally, or would you like to leave a detailed message on his or her voicemail?"**

4. **You faint from the shock.**

4.5 **You tell others.**

Press one if you hate voicemail. Press the hot button of the prospect if you want to get a call back and make the sale in spite of it. Press on.

If you do leave a message on someone's voicemail, ask yourself, "Would I return this call?"

If you hesitate to say *yes*, change your message.

Take a risk.
Take a chance.
Use your creativity.
Don't be afraid to make a mistake,
don't be afraid to fail, don't worry about
rejection, and don't quit just because
some yahoo won't see you.

Can't get an appointment?

The guy won't appoint me. I can't get an appointment. He didn't show for his appointment. He won't commit to an appointment. She won't return my phone call. He has rescheduled me three times in two weeks.

Welcome to the reality of a salesperson. The above situations are not problems – they are symptoms. When these symptoms (excuses) occur, there are unstated but obvious objections. Pick the one that applies to you.

If you think none of these apply to you, think again:

- You haven't established enough interest.
- You haven't given any value.
- You haven't created or uncovered need.
- You are unable to or have not established rapport.
- The prospect is already doing business with someone she is satisfied with.
- You have been talking (telling) instead of asking (selling).
- The prospect doesn't see you as important enough to carve out time to meet.
- The prospect feels "sale" rather than "relationship."
- The prospect has an unfavorable impression of you, your company, or your product.

Get creative, Jack (Jackie). You're not going to let little things like that prevent you from achieving your objective. Are you?

Here are some strategies and tactics that have worked:

- **Find someone you know who knows who you want to appoint.** Get this person to call Mr. Elusive for you if possible (to smooth the way, or find out the real reason he won't see you).

- **Use the fax.** Send a referral letter, a top 10 list, a cartoon, or your schedule for next week with the open times circled. Use the fax to open the door.

- **Send a plant, flowers, or a small gift.** You will be amazed how much ice you can melt with a small gift. Flowers can get through a brick wall no matter how thick it is. The right gift basket will bring a remarkable response.

- **Get close to the administrative person who knows your prospect best.** Find out what your prospect likes. His typical schedule – arrival and departure times. Gather information.

- **Arrange to meet the prospect at a networking event.** Trade association meeting, chamber of commerce event, ball game. Want to know where he'll be? Ask the prospect's administrative person or sales team.

- **Send a provocative letter without being provoking.** Ask questions or make statements in the letter that make the prospect think. Don't sell your product; just pique interest and sell an appointment.

- **Cold call at a time when you know (from the administrative person) he'll be there.** The best time is before the workday begins or after it is over.

- **Take a risk; take a chance.** Use your creativity. Don't be afraid to make a mistake, don't be afraid to fail, don't worry about rejection, and don't quit just because some yahoo won't see you. If you believe you can help the other person, never quit.

Free Git✗Bit... **There are benefits that transcend getting the appointment.** Using your creative power achieves four other purposes. To read the list, go to www.gitomer.com, register if you're a first-time visitor, and enter the words CREATIVE POWER in the GitBit box.

THE SALES BIBLE

Part 6
Woes and Foes

The Book of Lamentations

"You can't be a winner if you're a whiner… wiener."

– Jeffrey Gitomer

6.1

You don't have to sell it...
95% of the time the customer will buy it!

When bad sales happen to good people.

There's good and bad in all professions. Sales is no exception. Surveys show the only thing lower than a salesman in the minds of many Americans is a politician.

I got a call from a guy who said he went to a car dealer with cash wanting a new car. The salesman was so bad, he left without purchasing, still hasn't purchased, and has told 25 to 50 people how bad the experience was. Unfortunately this is far from an isolated experience. There are thousands of examples of poor salesmanship. But it isn't you. Is it?

Every business owner and sales pro reading this will swear, "It can't happen here." And they are dead wrong. Salespeople get cocky, think they know it all, think the customer is stupid or unwise to their tactics, treat everyone in the same manner, and end up losing the sale.

They fail to focus on the fundamental elements to position the customer or prospect for the buy. Relax – you don't always have to *sell* it. If you do it right, 95% of the time the customer will *buy* it!

Here are 10 common mistakes made by know-it-all salespeople (who actually know little or nothing at all):

1. Prejudging the prospect. Either by looks, dress, or speech, you have made up your mind what type of person this is and whether they have money or will buy.

2. Poor prospect qualification. Failure to ask the right questions about what the prospect wants or needs before the selling process begins.

3. Not listening. Concentrating on a *selling* angle instead of trying to understand how the prospect wants (needs) to *buy*.

4. Condescension. Acting or talking above (talking down to) the prospect. Making the buyer feel unequal in the selling/buying process. Lack of respect.

5. Pressure to buy today. If you have to resort to those tactics, it's because you are afraid the customer might find a better deal elsewhere. Also indicates a "no relationship" attitude.

6. Not addressing needs. If you listen to prospects, they will tell you exactly what they want or need. Sell back something that addresses those needs, and the prospect will buy. Don't sell in terms of you; sell in terms of the prospect.

7. Telegraphing closes and hard selling. "If I can get you this price, will you buy it today?" is a repulsive sales line reserved for salespeople in need of training, or salespeople who like losing sales. When you close, don't make it obvious.

8. Making the buyer doubt your intentions. If you change from friendly to pressure at the end of the presentation, or change terms or prices, the buyer loses confidence – and you lose the sale.

9. Lack of sincerity. *Sincerity is the key. If you can fake that, you've got it made,* is an old sales adage. It's half true. Sincerity is the key to building trust and establishing a relationship with a prospect who will become a customer if you are successful at conveying the feeling.

9.5 Poor attitude. "I'm doing you a favor by selling you. Don't ask me to go out of my way, because I won't."

Here is an easy self-test to determine if you are losing customers. Can you answer yes to these?

- Do I know my prospect's needs before I begin the selling process?
- Am I addressing the needs of the prospect during the sale?
- Do I look at the prospect when she is talking?
- Do I take notes and ask questions to strengthen my understanding?
- Would I buy from me if I were the customer?
- Am I sincere?

I hope you can answer no to these:

- Do I use (high) pressure tactics to get the customer to buy today?
- Do I have to resort to telling the customer about some sales contest or sob story to try to elicit the sale?
- Do I use antiquated sales tactics and think my prospect is too stupid to know?
- Do buyers doubt my intentions?
- Are contracts being canceled after the prospect goes home and thinks about it?

Failure is an event, not a person.
– Zig Ziglar
People aren't afraid of failure,
they just don't know how to succeed.
– Jeffrey Gitomer

18.5 characteristics of sales career failures.

You are responsible for your own success (or failure). Winning at a career in sales is no exception. To ensure a win, you must take a proactive approach. Prevention of failure is an important part of that process.

If you find yourself saying, "I'm not cut out for sales" or "I'm not pushy enough" or "I hate cold calling" or "I can't take the rejection" or "My boss is a jerk" or "My boss is a *real* jerk," you're heading down the wrong path.

Here are 18.5 recurring characteristics and traits of people who thought they could hit a home run in a sales career. But they struck out in their attempt – many of them with their bat on their shoulder – failing to swing at the ball as it passed them by for a called third strike. How many of these apply to you?

1. YOU DON'T BELIEVE IN YOURSELF. If you don't think you can do it, who will?

2. YOU DON'T BELIEVE IN YOUR PRODUCT. Failure to believe that your product or service is the best will show. Lack of conviction is evident to a buyer and manifests itself in low sales numbers.

3. FAILURE TO SET AND ACHIEVE GOALS. FAILURE TO PLAN. Failure to define and achieve specific long-term (what you want) and short-term (how you're going to get what you want) goals.

4. YOU'RE LAZY ("SLACK" IN THE SOUTH) OR JUST NOT PREPARED TO MAKE THE SALE. Your self-motivation and preparation are the lifeblood of your outreach. You must be eager and ready to sell, or you won't.

5. FAILURE TO UNDERSTAND HOW TO ACCEPT REJECTION. They're not rejecting you; they're just rejecting the offer you're making them.

6. FAILURE TO MASTER THE TOTAL KNOWLEDGE OF YOUR PRODUCT (failure to know your product cold). Total product knowledge gives you the mental freedom to concentrate on selling.

7. FAILURE TO LEARN AND EXECUTE THE FUNDAMENTALS OF SALES. Read, listen to CDs, attend seminars, and practice what you've just learned. Everything you need to know about sales has already been written or spoken. Learn something new every day.

8. FAILURE TO UNDERSTAND THE CUSTOMER AND MEET HIS OR HER NEEDS. Failure to question and listen to the prospect and uncover true needs. Includes prejudging prospects.

9. FAILURE TO OVERCOME OBJECTIONS. This is a complex issue. You are not listening to the prospect; you are not thinking in terms of solution; you are not able to create an atmosphere of confidence and trust suitable enough to cause (effect) a sale.

10. CAN'T COPE WITH CHANGE. Part of sales is change. Change in products, tactics, and markets. Roll with it to succeed. Fight it and fail.

11. CAN'T FOLLOW RULES. Salespeople think rules are made for others. Think they're not for you? Think again. Broken rules will only get you fired.

12. CAN'T GET ALONG WITH OTHERS (co-workers and customers). Sales is never a solo effort. You must team with your co-workers and partner with your customers.

13. TOO DAMN GREEDY. Selling for commissions instead of helping customers.

14. FAILURE TO DELIVER WHAT YOU PROMISED. Failure to do what you say you're going to do, either for your company or your customer, is a disaster from which you may never recover. If you do it, word will get out about you.

15. FAILURE TO ESTABLISH LONG-TERM RELATIONSHIPS. Trying to make commissions leads to failure through insincerity, failure by lack of service, and failure to be motivated by anything but money.

16. FAILURE TO UNDERSTAND THAT HARD WORK MAKES LUCK. Take a close look at the people you think are lucky. They (or someone in their family) put in years of hard work to create that luck. You can get just as lucky.

17. BLAMING OTHERS WHEN THE FAULT (OR RESPONSIBILITY) IS YOURS. Accepting responsibility is the fulcrum point of succeeding at anything. Doing something about it is the criterion. Execution is the reward (not the money – money is just the by-product of perfect execution).

18. LACK OF PERSISTENCE. You are willing to take no for an answer and just accept it without a fight. You are unable to motivate the prospect to act, or are unwilling to persist through the 7 to 10 exposures it takes to make the sale.

18.5 FAILURE TO ESTABLISH AND MAINTAIN A POSITIVE ATTITUDE. The first rule of life.

If you're weak in any one of the above 18.5 areas, it's urgent that you make a change. Sales weaknesses are like cancer. Mostly self-inflicted due to bad habits and neglect, easy to uncover, and hard to cure – but not impossible. It takes outside help and regular treatments to maintain excellent sales health.

Failure is not about insecurity. It's about lack of execution. There's no such thing as a total failure.

There are degrees of failing. Here are 4.5 of them:

1. **Failing to do your best.**
2. **Failing to learn.**
3. **Failing to accept responsibility.**
4. **Failing to meet quotas or pre-set goals.**
4.5 **Failing to have a positive attitude.**

What degree are you?

*"The reason I never made buckets of money for the
company is because nobody ever gave me a bucket!"*

The
Book of
Competition

"Of course
you know, this
means WAR."
— *Bugs Bunny/
Groucho Marx*

Competition...

Gentlemen,
start your sales pitch.

To the victor go the sales.
All's fair in love and sales.
I'm in the mood for sales.

Carl Lewis won the 100-meter dash three Olympics in a row. Who came in second? Who cares?

Are you going for the gold, or will you come in second?

There's no prize for second place in sales.

When you're in a foot race with your competition, here's what to do...

Dancing with the competition? Watch your step.

How do you feel about your competitors? You say, "I have a great relationship with my competitors."

Right, if you needed $50,000 or your business would fold, I guarantee your *friend* the competitor would send you a *bon voyage* note.

Get real. Competitors may talk to you, they may be civil to you, and they may even appear to help you – but ask them if they wish you were dead or alive, and I'm betting on the funeral home.

They help me, they send me business, they call me to discuss common problems, there's enough business for everyone – all are statements your competitors are hoping you'll say while they systematically plan to destroy you. That's life in the jungle of business (and especially sales).

Friendly competition – there's a good one. "Now let's play fair. I got the last sale, so you can have this one." I don't think so. Friendly competition is kinda like friendly snakes. They'll turn and bite you in a heartbeat, and it's *real tricky* to tell the poisonous ones from the safe ones.

Competition is a lot like an unknown snake. Potentially poisonous, not someone you want to get real close to, it's best to know all you can about them, respect 'em, and always carry a snake bite kit with you – just in case.

Facts about the competition and their feelings about you:
- Some are OK.
- Some will cooperate.
- Some are ethical.
- Some like competition.
- Some will like you.
- Some will trade business with you.
- Some will help you.
- Most won't. Most don't like you.

How to deal with competition:
- Know where they stand in the market.
- Know who their major customers are.
- Are they taking business from you, or are you taking business from them?
- Have they captured any of your employees?
- Get every piece of their information (sales literature, brochures).
- Get their prices.
- Shop them every quarter. Know how they sell and what they feature.
- Identify where they are weaker than you and play on it.
- Learn where they are stronger than you and fix it ... IMMEDIATELY.

When you are up against competition on a sales call:
- Never say anything bad about them, even if the prospect does.
- Praise them as worthy competition.
- Show them respect.
- Show how you differ – how your benefits are better.
- Stress your strengths, not their weaknesses.
- Show a testimonial from a customer who switched to you.
- Maintain your ethics and professionalism at all times – even if it means biting your tongue until it bleeds.

"Competition
does not
mean war.
It means learn.
It means prepare.
It means
be your best."

–Jeffrey Gitomer

The Book of Customer Service

"To serve is to rule."

– Lao Tzu

Are you serving others the way you expect to be served?

Make your customer happy. Keep your customer happy. Forever.

If you don't have the time or the interest to do so, someone else will.

Sell them and serve them so that you can sell them again.
And again.

Where does customer service begin? In the next decade, it will BEGIN with a 100% loyal customer. Start now.

Don't let your customers sing "I can't get no satisfaction."

Here's how to create memorable, legendary customer service…

7.1

Satisfactory customer service
is no longer acceptable.

The secret of great customer service.

Customer service is one of the most maligned terms in our language. So often as customers, you're disappointed in the service you receive (or the attitude attached to the service), that you go elsewhere. Amazing. The company made the sale, got the customer, and then – through an act of rudeness, indifference, poor follow-up, bad service, or slow response – lost the customer it fought so hard (and spent so much) to get.

Seems ridiculous, but it happens thousands of times every day. It's happened to you many times. And, boy, do you talk about it. In fact, statistics show a disgruntled customer tells 20 times more people than a satisfied one.

How good is your customer service? Once you make the sale, are you as intense to keep the customer as you were to get the customer?

I attended a Ty Boyd seminar called "The Spirit of Customer Service." I thought I was going to get a great lesson from a great speaker. I was wrong. I got an unbelievable series of lessons from a master presenter. I was rewarded with more than 100 rules, lessons, and examples about what to do and what NOT to do in the never-ending quest to serve (and preserve) the customer.

How do you lose customers? Ty offers the Seven Deadly Sins of Service:

1. **Putting money or profits ahead of service.**
2. **Complacency brought about by success (getting fat).**
3. **Organizational layering without creating teamwork (people blaming others or whining "It's not my job").**
4. **Lack of proper employee training, recognition, or retention.**
5. **Not listening – Anticipating the answer before hearing the situation.**
6. **Isolationism – Not paying attention to the customer or the competition.**
7. **Lip service, or worse, lying.**

You have probably been victims of every one of these sins at one time or another. Yet if I ask you if you commit any of these, you'll say *NO.* Guess what? Someone's lying or living in fantasy land.

Customer service is a complex issue critical to the ongoing success of any business. *It's easy to go astray without guidelines and standards.*

Here is some of Ty Boyd's wisdom about customer service:
- **Satisfactory customer service is no longer acceptable.**
- **Customer service begins at 100%.**
- **The customer's perception is reality.**
- **A mistake is a chance to improve the company.**
- **Problems can create beneficial rearrangements.**
- **Make the customer feel important.**
- **Learn how to ask questions.**
- **The most important art – the art of listening.**

Ty spoke in detail about refining the skill of listening. It's a vital key in the customer service process. As salespeople, you're prone to talk way too much. Sometimes you lose sales and customers because you fail to hear their true needs and desires.

Ty offered the following rules to maximize your listening skills and increase customer loyalty:

1. **Don't interrupt.** ("But … but … but …")

2. **Ask questions, then be quiet.** Concentrate on really listening.

3. **Prejudice will distort what you hear.** Listen without prejudging.

4. **Don't jump to answer before you hear the ENTIRE situation.**

5. **Listen for purpose, details, and conclusions.**

6. **Active listening involves interpreting.**

7. **Listen to what is not said.** What is implied is often more important than what is spoken.

8. **Think between sentences.**

9. **Digest what is said (and not said) before engaging your mouth.**

10. **Demonstrate you are listening by taking action.**

Sounds simple – it is! Just focus on it.

Outstanding customer service is a powerful sales tool.

Customer service is the never-ending pursuit of excellence to gain a level of loyalty in which customers tell others of the way they were treated in your place of business.

Is that the way your customers feel? If they do, you're among 5% of American businesses. The other 95% fall short of that mark, according to Ty Boyd. For years, Ty has compiled information and spoken worldwide on customer service.

Every business has a different definition of customer service because of the diverse types of their products and services. The constants among them are the attributes of customer service.

Here are Ty's 12 key attributes of customer service – how many are present in your company?

1. Dedication to customer satisfaction by *every* employee in the company.
2. Immediate response to the customer (now, not tomorrow).
3. Individuals taking responsibility for customers' needs (no buck passing).
4. Do what you say and follow up immediately.
5. Agreement with, and empathy for, the complaint or situation of the customer.
6. Flexibility to serve specific needs of individual customers (the ability to go beyond *policy*).
7. An empowerment of employees to decide.
8. Consistent on-time delivery.
9. Deliver what you promise before AND after the sale.
10. A *zero-defects* and *error-free* delivery program.
11. Outstanding people to serve customers and implement customer service.
12. Smile when talking on the phone.

"Write down and live your customer service standards,"
says Ty Boyd (*passionately*).

AUTO ZONE. Strives to provide WOW! customer service and they live up to it. They have a GOTTCha program – *Get Out To The Customer's Car and Assist.* And they use the WITTDTJR philosophy – *What It Takes To Do The Job Right.* Do you? Auto Zone has high-energy, knowledgeable employees dedicated to greeting and helping customers, and a special emphasis on helping women feel informed about the products they need. Their stores are alive and customers can feel it.

NORDSTROM. Their entire service policy to employees is: *"Use your good judgment in all situations."* Seminar attendees who had shopped there cited example after example of service way beyond the call of duty, including going to competitors to buy products they are out of or don't stock and delivering them to customers at no additional charge.

L.L. BEAN. Before an employee can say *no* to a customer, he or she must have senior management approval. Think about that.

The philosophy is simple...Legendary service builds fortunes in repeat customers. Poor service will drive your customers to your competition.

Every time you encounter a customer, try this...Measure the value (and profit) of a customer over 10 years, and you begin to look at them in a whole new way.

Ty has written a list of *51 Ways to Get Closer to the Real Boss, Your Customer.* Here are a few samples:

- **Have top management people make sales calls regularly.**

- **Install a customer *hot line*.**

- **Make it a policy to return all inquiry or complaint calls within 1 hour.**

- **Set a goal to resolve every complaint within 24 hours ... then shorten it to 12 hours.**

- **Have your top staff/management personally answer complaints.**

- **Create a slogan centered around "[Our Company] means SERVICE." Put it on your walls, on your letterhead, on your literature, on uniforms. Tattoo it on your forehead.**

When a customer has a complaint,
you have an opportunity
to solidify your relationship.

Customer complaints breed sales. If you handle them correctly.

The customer is always right. Except when he or she is wrong, which is most of the time. In sales, right and wrong don't matter. It's the perception of the customer that matters. Keeping the customer satisfied and happy is what matters. What's the best method of handling the dreaded customer complaint? Try the *Personal Touch Method*.

The Personal Touch Method is a strategy I developed and have used over and over. To institute this method, you must first *take responsibility* – even if the fault isn't yours or you won't be the one who handles it. The customer doesn't care. He's pissed. He wants *you* to handle it. Now.

Here are 14.5 steps to taking responsibility when dealing with an unhappy or dissatisfied customer:

1. **Tell them you understand how they feel.**

2. **Empathize with them. (Cite a similar situation. Tell them that it makes you mad too. Tell them a similar thing happened to you.)**

3. **Listen all the way out. Make sure customers have told you everything. Don't interrupt. Ask questions to understand the problem better and to find out what it will take to satisfy them.**

4. **Agree with them if at all possible. (Never argue or get angry.)**

5. Take notes and confirm back that everything has been covered, and that they have said all they want/need to say.

6. Be an ambassador for your company. Tell the customer you will personally handle it.

7. Don't blame others or look for a scapegoat. Admit you (and/or the company) were wrong and take responsibility for correcting it.

8. Don't pass the buck. "It's not my job," … "I thought he said," … "She's not here right now," … and "Someone else handles that" are responses that are never applicable or acceptable to the customer.

9. Respond immediately. When something is wrong, people want (and expect) it to be fixed immediately. The customer wants it perfect.

10. Find some common ground other than the problem. (Try to establish some rapport.)

11. Use humor if possible. Making people laugh puts them at ease.

12. Figure out, communicate, and agree upon a solution or resolve. Give customers choices if possible. Confirm it (in writing if necessary). Tell them what you plan to do, and DO IT!

13. Make a follow-up call after the situation is resolved.

14. Get a letter if you can. Resolving a problem in a favorable and positive way strengthens respect, builds character, and establishes a solid base for long-term relationships. Tell the customer you would appreciate a sentence or two about how the situation was resolved.

14.5 Ask yourself: "What have I learned, and what can I do to prevent this situation from happening again? Do I need to make changes?"

RECOVERY IS POWERFUL. When you satisfy an unhappy or dissatisfied customer, and you can get him or her to write a letter telling you that you resolved the issue, you have a solid shot at a long-term relationship.

If the problem is left unresolved, the customer will surely find your competition.

It is important to be aware of some practical realities when trying to accomplish the task of satisfying the customer:

- The customer knows exactly how they want it, or exactly what they want, but may be a lousy communicator and not tell you completely, or tell you in a way that is difficult to understand. If the customer cannot state his complaint in a clear and concise manner, it's up to you to help him do so.

- Remember, you're the customer elsewhere. Think about the level of service you expect when you're the customer.

- Every customer thinks he's the only one you've got. Treat him that way. Make the customer feel important.

- The customer is human and has problems just like we do.

- The customer expects service at the flip of a switch.

- It all boils down to you.

- The customer's perception is reality.

- How big a deal is it to try to give customers what they want?

*"When you say 'satisfaction guaranteed,'
do you mean my satisfaction or yours?"*

THE SALES BIBLE

Part 8
Spreading the Gospel

The Book of Communications

Say What?

Communication is the lifeblood of the selling process.

Communication is not just talking.

It's getting your mission accomplished by a combination of
talking,
writing,
listening,
and doing.

Complete communication with your prospects, your customers, and your associates must be your purpose.

Talk it up,
listen up,
do it up,
so you can write it up.

Communication = Sales!

8.1

Make an appointment
one minute after your sales meeting.
You'll be pumped.
Why not take it out on a prospect?

A weekly sales meeting is a place to create new sales.

Sales caffeine. The early morning sales meeting.

Sales staff meetings are a vital link between what your company expects the sales team to do and what actually gets sold in the trenches. It's a place where marketing is converted to sales. But how often is the opportunity provided by these meetings lost? Answer: Too often.

Sales meetings should be a forum for reporting, goal achievement assistance, encouragement, problem solving, training, sharing, and communication. The purpose of a sales meeting is to get the sales staff primed and pumped to sell.

NOTE: I've left two things off the menu. Whining and complaining. They're not allowed.

Last week I attended a well-designed Monday morning sales meeting.
- **They had an agenda and stuck to it.**
- **Each member of the staff had an opportunity to talk about their best sale of the past week.**
- **There was a sales lesson.**
- **There was very little administrative stuff.**
- **There was 15 minutes of product knowledge.**

WANT TO RATE YOUR WEEKLY SALES MEETING: Ask yourself this question: If the meeting were not mandatory, would you go?

The two-hour meeting kept the staff involved and in learning mode. It was one of the rare sales meetings I have attended that produced no gripes and great sales information.

How do you have a great sales meeting every time? Preplanning and preparation. Let lots of people have their chance to lead. Set an agenda that will work, be fun, be productive, include participation by everyone, and STICK TO IT.

Here are some criteria to consider:

- **Very little administration.** Five minutes tops.

- **Don't do boring things** like go over new forms, company policy, personal disputes, and what went wrong. Figure out a better, faster way to communicate. Try this – have an instruction sheet for the new form and just pass it out. CLUE: Salespeople don't pay attention to administrivia anyway.

- **Don't present problems unless you have thought of some solutions to go with them.** This rule applies to everyone. It gets people solution oriented.

- **Do fun things that help salespeople feel good about themselves.** Awards; share success stories.

- **Do things that help salespeople learn more about their profession.** Have a mini-lesson on one topic per week. Have it prepared and presented by one of the sales team.

- **Do things that help salespeople earn more money.** Thrash out objections and obstacles that create roundtable discussion. Role-play solutions.

- **Bring in people from the real world.** Have one customer attend each week and tell why he or she buys from you. You'll be amazed, but this is a powerful dose of reality. The customer will dissect the BUYING process (way more powerful than you trying to learn the SELLING process).

- **Have meetings early in the morning.** Have great food and great coffee ready early.

- **Make people be on time.** Fine late ones/reward early ones. START ON TIME no matter what, and END ON TIME no matter what.

- **Stress the positive.** Support your people in public, especially among peers. If you have a negative about an individual, say it to him or her privately.

A sales meeting is a place to plan this week's sales. Some people use the forum to threaten and complain; some use it to encourage and learn – guess who wins?

Get to the point in the first sentence.

The sales letter will work, if you get it *write*.

How important is a sales letter?

I have received hundreds of sales letters of all different types. Introduction, literature enclosed, just met you, after the presentation, follow-up, here's the information, thanks for the order – you get the idea. Most have a specific purpose. Most are not very good (uninspiring). OK. Most of them are *pathetic*.

The skill of drafting *sales words* on a letter is an integral part of the sales process because it creates an impression of you and your company when the customer or prospect reads it.

HERE'S HOW IT WORKS: If you write a great letter, they think you're great. If you write a creative letter, they think you're creative. If you write a dumb letter...

Some salespeople have a hard time coming up with the appropriate words. Not because they can't write, but because they don't know the rules of writing.

Here are some guidelines to help turn your sales letters into sales:

1. **State your objective or the purpose of your letter in the first sentence.** Get to the point. You can even use a headline above the body of the text.
2. **Use short paragraphs.** For emphasis.
3. **Edit, edit, edit.** Take out every word not integral to the purpose or objective of the communication.
4. **Keep the letter short.** One page. Three paragraphs. The shorter it is, the better chance you have of the letter being read and understood.

5. **Don't make the prospect vomit when he or she reads your letter.** Make the letter easy to digest. Avoid heavy syrup. Half the adjectives, half the prepositional phrases. Eliminate most adverbs. Look behind commas to see if the entire phrase is worthy of keeping. Most of the time, it's not.

6. **Use bullets to break up the monotony.**
   - Make the letter easy to read graphically.
   - Use bullets to emphasize the most important points.

7. **Don't say "Thank you for the opportunity."** Instead try, "I'm proud to offer."

8. **Don't bold your name.** Bold what's important to the prospect. Your name is among the least important in the letter.

9. **Don't make it sound like a rubber stamp.**

10. **Don't sell your product too much.** Sell the next action step in the sales cycle and build confidence and rapport.

11. **Don't use the letter as a sales pitch.** Use it as a sales tool.

12. **Do the extra - the unexpected.** Enclose an article or something that pertains to the customer's business. Something that makes the prospect think you went beyond the norm to serve and communicate.

13. **Personalize it.** The more your letter relates to the other person's business and situation, the better they're going to feel about doing business with you.

14. **Solidify the next contact or event.** Date it and time it.

15. **Hand write whatever you can.**

16. **Avoid words that end in "ly."**

17. **Never say "again, thanks."** It's not necessary to thank anyone again. Once is enough, twice is groveling.

18. **Use a nice, non-begging, professional closing.** "Thank you for your time and consideration. I'll call you Tuesday."

19. **Sign your first name only.**

19.5 **Very truly yours (and I mean that), Jeffrey Gitomer.**

P.S. If you want to make your plea or point twice, use a P.S.

HERE'S A TOUGH RULE: Let your letter sit for a day, then re-read it. How does it sound to you? If the answer is thin or hokey, you may want to start over.

HERE IS A TOUGHER RULE: Ask someone *smart and impartial* to critique your letter. Learn to accept criticism, and use it as a learning tool.

HERE'S THE TOUGHEST RULE: Ask yourself how this letter would be different from your competition. Suppose the sale was based on the originality of your cover letter. Would you ever make another sale? Uh oh.

Knowing the rules and practicing them will lead to effective letters. Effective letters lead to prospect rapport and confidence. Prospect rapport and confidence lead to sales.

Free Git Bit...**Want a list of 51 Ways to Get Closer to The Real Boss, Your Customer?** Go to www.gitomer.com, register if you're a first-time visitor, and enter the words REAL BOSS in the GitBit box.

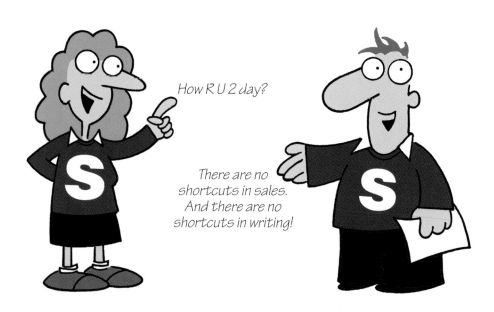

*Listening is arguably the most important
aspect of the selling process,
yet it's usually the weakest part
of a sales professional's skills.*

Want to close more sales?
Listen more closely!

Have you ever had a course in listening skills?

How to listen lessons were never offered as part of any formal education. It's amazing to me that the skills needed most for personal success were never taught in school.

Listening is arguably the most important aspect of the selling process, yet it's usually the weakest part of a sales professional's skills.

You listen to TV, radio, and CDs, and you can recite chapter and verse the next day, or sing the songs word for word. But if your spouse or child says something to you, you say, "What?" or "I didn't hear you."

How often do you ask people to repeat what they said? How often do you hear, "You weren't listening to a word I said." There are reasons for poor listening, and thank goodness I'm writing them down! Otherwise you'd be forced to listen and you know how effective that would be.

Here are the fundamental listening lessons:

LISTEN LESSON #1. *The two biggest impediments to listening are:*

1. **You often have an opinion (of you or what you're going to say) before you begin listening.**

2. **You often have made up your mind before you begin listening, or before you hear the full story.**

LISTEN LESSON #2. *The two important rules of effective listening must be observed in this order or you will not be an effective listener.*

1. First, listen with the intent to understand.
2. Second, listen with the intent to respond.

LISTEN LESSON #3. *Think about the way you listen right now:*

- Are you doing something else when someone is speaking?
- Do you have your mind on something else when someone is speaking?
- Do you fake listening so that you can get in your comments?
- Are you waiting for a pause to get in your response, because you already know the answer?

LISTEN LESSON #4. *At some point you stop listening. When does that occur?*

- After you have formulated your response.
- After you have been turned off by the speaker.
- When you decide to interrupt someone to say something.
- When the person speaking isn't saying anything you want to hear.

LISTEN LESSON #4.5 *What causes people not to listen?*

- Sometimes people are afraid to hear what is about to be said, so they block it out. Don't be afraid to listen.
- Sometimes you take the other person for granted – spouse, parent, child.
- Sometimes you're mentally preoccupied with other things.
- Sometimes you're just rude.
- Sometimes the person grates on you, so you don't listen.
- Sometimes you have other things on your mind.
- Sometimes you know the person speaking and have prejudged them.
- Sometimes you don't respect the other person and block the listening process.
- Sometimes you think you already know what is about to be said.
- Sometimes you think you know it all... or is that all the time?

LISTEN LESSON GUIDELINES. *Here are 14.5 guidelines to observe that will maximize your listening skills, increase your productivity, reduce errors, gain customer happiness, and help you make more sales:*

1. Don't interrupt. (But ... but ... but ...)
2. Ask questions. Then be (veweey, veweey) quiet. Concentrate on the other person's answers, not your thoughts.
3. Prejudice will distort what you hear. Listen without prejudging.
4. Use eye contact and listening noises (um, gee, I see, oh) to show the other person you're listening.
5. Don't jump to the answer before you hear the ENTIRE situation.
6. Listen for purpose, details, and conclusions.
7. Active listening involves interpreting. Interpret quietly or take notes.
8. Listen also to what is not said. Implied is often more important than spoken. HINT: Tone of speech will often reflect implied meaning.
9. Think between sentences and during quiet times.
10. Digest what is said (and not said) before engaging your mouth.
11. Ask questions to be sure you understood what was said or meant.
12. Ask questions to be sure the speaker said all he or she wanted to say.
13. Demonstrate you are listening by taking action.
14. If you're thinking during speaking, think solution. Don't embellish the problem.
14.5 Avoid all distractions. Turn off the cell and pager. Close the door. Clear your mind, and both sit or both stand in close proximity.

There are many secrets
to becoming a good
listener, but the one
that encompasses them
all is: Just shut up!

*A person who seems to have all
the answers usually isn't listening.*

Learn to listen in
two words. Shut up!

It's amazing how much you can learn by just keeping quiet. People think you're smarter if you're quiet. You learn more by listening than by speaking.

Effective listening leads to sales – lots of them. Listening is arguably the most important aspect of the selling process, yet it's the weakest part of a sales professional's skills.

How well do you listen?

Answer each statement *Rarely – Sometimes –* or *Always*:

R S A I allow speakers to complete sentences.
R S A I make sure I understand the other person's point of view before responding.
R S A I listen for the important points.
R S A I try to understand the speaker's feelings.
R S A I visualize the solution before speaking.
R S A I visualize my response before speaking.
R S A I am in control, relaxed, and calm when listening.
R S A I use listening noises ("um," "gee," "I see," "oh").
R S A I take notes when someone else is speaking.
R S A I listen with an open mind.
R S A I listen even if the other person is not interesting.
R S A I listen even if the other person is a jerk.
R S A I look at the person I'm listening to.
R S A I am patient when I listen.
R S A I ask questions to be sure I understand.
R S A I have no distractions when I listen.

How you rate as an effective listener. How many always did you get?

14 - 16   You're excellent.

11 - 13   You're good, but need help in a few areas.

 7 - 10   You're fair, probably think you know it all, and could increase your income significantly with skill-building help.

 4 - 6   You're poor, not listening at all.

 1 - 3   You're ear dead or brain dead or in need of a hearing aid.

Turn any of the above listening weaknesses into listening goals by substituting "I will" for "I," or "I will be" for "I am."

For example: If you answered Sometimes for "I allow speakers to complete sentences," you can make that a goal by writing "I will allow speakers to complete all sentences for the next 30 days" on a Post-It Note and putting it up on your bathroom mirror.

Shhh...Effective listening requires regularly practiced skill-building ideas. Here are 17.5 you can practice:

1. **Look right at the person you're listening to.**

2. **Focus your attention on the words and their meaning.**

3. **Limit distractions (even change locations to listen better).**

4. **Visualize the situation being described to you.**

5. **Visualize your response or solution before responding.**

6. **Listen with an open mind. No prelistening prejudice.**

7. **Listen to the content – not necessarily how it's being delivered.**

8. **Use occasional listening noises or "Wow" or "Gosh" or "Then what?" or "Really" or "That's horrible" or "Great" or "That's too bad" or "I didn't know that" or "I see."**

9. **Write things down as others are speaking. Jot down a word rather than interrupt the other person's thought...**
   - **To keep the thought.**
   - **To impress the other person.**
   - **To be polite.**
   - **To keep listening instead of interrupting.**

10.   Verify the situation (sometimes) before giving feedback.

11.   Qualify the situation with questions before giving feedback or responding.

12.   Don't interrupt the next time you think you know the answer.

13.   Go for an hour without speaking.

14.   Next time you eat with a group, don't talk for the first half hour.

15.   Ask questions to clarify.

16.   Ask questions to show interest or concern.

17.   Ask questions to get more information or learn.

17.5 Ask yourself, "Are you listening to the other person the same way you want to be listened to?"

LOOK OUT FOR POOR LISTENERS: A person who seems to have all the answers usually isn't listening. A person who interrupts isn't listening (or at least is not a good listener).

HOW HARD IS IT TO LISTEN? For some people it's impossible.

Listening is the toughest lesson for me to give. First, because I'm often a poor listener myself. Almost every sale I ever lost I can attribute to poor listening or poor questioning. Second, because I can't change in one or two chapters what took 20 years to create.

TEST YOUR LISTENING SELF-DISCIPLINE: Try being silent for one hour. Try not talking in a group of people. Try not talking at a party.

Listen with the intent to understand, before you listen with the intent to respond.

There are no such things as buyer types,
only buyer characteristics.
No two buyers are alike.

There are 100 billion buyer types. Go figure.

Selling is not about defining the type of buyer you're facing. There are billions of types of buyers. Ever see those "four types of buyer" things? The Driver. The Amiable. The Idiot. The Big Idiot. The Big Idiot is someone who thinks there are four types of people and you can somehow pigeonhole them into characteristic categories that will make them buy. Bogus.

I'll give you three words that will let you absolutely identify every type of buyer in the world in five minutes:

    1. Look (around the office)

    2. Question (the right questions)

    3. Listen (with the intent to understand)

There. The *Gitomer Method* of identifying more than 100 billion buyer types reduced to three words. These are the methods used in determining customer characteristics. Oh yeah – there's one more thing you need to do to get it right every time.

Practice!

Selling is knowledge combined with experience. The knowledge you gain about your product, your selling skills, and your attitude. Experience teaches you how to implement the knowledge you've gained. It's a science, remember? Trial and error. Of course there are some absolute rules that can never be broken: Don't argue. Don't lie. But most are shades of gray.

How much pressure do you apply? Someone will say none; someone else wrote a book about hardball selling – it comes with a bat. The amount of pressure is up to you!

There are no buyer types – there are buyer characteristics. Individual traits that make up a personality. Don't categorize them. Understand them.

I'm way more interested in buyers' philosophies than their characteristics. But I can only get to their philosophy if I recognize (and understand) their traits. If you've uncovered their "type," but you've said something that they're philosophically opposed to, you're dead.

Why do customers buy?

- **To solve a problem.**
- **They need it.**
- **They think they need it.**
- **To get a competitive edge.**
- **To save money or produce faster.**
- **To eliminate mistakes or people.**
- **To feel good.**
- **To show off.**
- **To change a mood.**
- **To solidify a relationship.**
- **They were talked into it.**
- **It sounded too good to refuse.**
- **They got a great deal (or thought they did).**

How many of these characteristics apply to the buyers you face?

- **The tire kicker**
- **The liar**
- **The logical**
- **The indecisive**
- **The unfriendly**
- **The impulsive**
- **The know-it-all**
- **The Yankee**
- **The faithful**
- **The friendly – won't commit**
- **The impolite**
- **The ounce of power**
- **The price-only buyer**
- **The bragger**
- **The arguer**
- **The no-talker**
- **The emotional**
- **The "think it over"**

- The unqualified
- The talker
- The hidden objection
- The procrastinator
- The rude
- The cheapskate
- The good ole boy
- The corpse

These characteristics are identified one by one – BUT your buyer is a combination of several of these and other traits.

FOR EXAMPLE: The good-ole-boy, tire-kicker, price-buyer, think-it-over... that's a prospect who can make a Yankee salesperson go looking for a U-Haul trailer to move back north. Or how about the Yankee-know-it-all, unfriendly, liar? That's a prospect that would make a Southern salesperson want to go rent him one.

Here are a few guidelines that will work on any type of buyer:

1. Never argue.
2. Never offend.
3. Never think or act like you're defeated.
4. Try to make a friend at all costs.
5. Try to get on the same side of the fence (harmonize).
6. Never tell a lie.

THERE'S A THEME HERE. A common thread that connects all these situations. One word makes all these types conquerable: HARMONIZE. If you listen to buyers and watch their actions, they will tell you how to react. They will tell you what to say and what not to say. They will lead you to the sale. Your job is to take the characteristics of the prospect and blend them with the reason the prospect is buying so that it motivates the prospect to act, and gives the prospect enough confidence to buy. Simple.

There are billions of "customer types." Want to sell them all? You can do it in five words: Look. Question. Listen. Harmonize. Practice.

Free Git✗Bit...When someone talks to you, updates you on a project, asks you to do something, assigns you a task, has a business communication of any kind, or just needs a favor – want to know the method that eliminates misunderstanding and errors? Go to www.gitomer.com, register if you're a first-time visitor, and enter the words ERROR FREE COMMUNICATION in the GitBit box.

"There are billions of 'customer types.' Want to sell them all? You can do it in five words:

Look. Question. Listen. Harmonize. Practice."

— *Jeffrey Gitomer*

The Book of Exhibitions

Showing Off

Exhibitions...

Remember
"Show and Tell"?
This is the adult version
of the game.

It's called "Show and Sell."

Where else can you be face-
to-face with thousands of
prospects over the course of
a few days?

Everyone is there
to do business.

Fish in a barrel.
Thousands of them.

All you need is a hook.

I'll supply the bait...

It's your annual convention...
You can see a concentration of people in your industry.
Nowhere else can you see this many
customers and prospects at once.
You have no time to waste.

35.5 trade show success rules.

It's time for your annual business fair, trade show, or convention. Hundreds of your customers, prospects, suppliers, and competitors will be in town for two days. Nowhere else can you see such a concentration of people in your industry. It's about opportunity – selling, prospecting, and relationship building. How will you take advantage of it?

It's also about time, and the proper use of it. If 7,500 people will attend over a two-day, 20-hour span, what does that mean to you? And what should you do about it? How do you capitalize on this event?

Some people go to conventions because it's a chance to get away from the office, get out of town, or have a good time. If you want to be successful, steer clear of these people.

Here are 35.5 ideas to help you plan for and maximize your benefit from the next convention you attend. These success rules and observations will help you work the show and understand its power:

1. Think. How long does it take you to make 7,500 sales calls anyplace other than a trade show? At 20 a day – which is a lot of (outside) calls – it would take you 375 days (1.5 work years) to make 7,500 sales calls. Wow. If you telemarketed 125 calls a day, it would take you 60 days to make 7,500 calls. Wow.

2. Taking advantage of a trade show, the most cost-effective sales opportunity of the year, requires preparation. Lots of it. You better be ready to win if you expect to win. Be ready with your exhibit, your stuff, your staff. Be prepared with your pitch; have your information at your command. Have your presentation material ready and rehearsed. Have power questions and power statements ready. Your opening line and presentation statements must be perfect.

3. Develop your game plan before you leave your office. Have a set of goals and objectives for the number of prospects you want to secure, customers you want to visit, sales you want to make, and how you intend to accomplish the tasks.

4. Stay at the main/best hotel. Be in the middle of what's happening. It may cost a few bucks more, but it's worth it.

5. Get there a day early. You will have the advantage of being relaxed and up to the minute on things of importance. Many convention exhibitors and attendees will be flying in on your plane. Try to find them.

6. Work the trade show during setup. If you're not an exhibitor, somehow get in. Go to the truck entrance; tell them you're delivering an important part or paper, but get in. Walking the trade show early gives you a tactical advantage and may net you some valuable contacts. Many company CEOs like to be there when the booth is being set up. It's a relaxed time to get in some valuable contact time without being rushed.

7. Target five important people in your industry you want to get to know, and make it your business to seek them out and talk to them.

8. Target 10 customers. Connect. Build relationships. Take them to dinner. Solidify your position as a vendor.

9. Target 10 prospects. Connect. Build rapport for a sale later.

10. Find out about every hospitality suite and after-hours party being given. Target the ones where your prospects are most likely to be. Go there.

11. Be the first to arrive and the last to leave every day. This has been most successful for me. It gives me an edge on the people who get there late and leave early. One or two extra hours can mean another 100 contacts.

12. Be a team. Split the responsibilities. If more than one person is attending from your company, split up and assign responsibilities.

13. Attend seminars and lectures where you can network with your customers and prospects. Sitting next to the right person in a seminar can be very beneficial. If you meet a prospect or customer, ask what seminars they plan to attend. Be there.

14. Be a presenter. Give a talk or seminar that will establish your expertise and position you or your company as a leader in your field.
Pick a topic that your customer or prospect is likely to attend.

15. Stay focused. Look for opportunities where you least expect them. In the lobby, in the elevator, in the rest room, in the restaurant – be alert for opportunity. You're going to be face-to-face with decision makers and people who influence them.

16. Sell everywhere. No place is off-limits. Aisles, other booths, bathrooms, food stands – be on alert for the people you're looking to meet. Read badges. Talk and look (without being rude). You never know when you'll bump into a major prospect (or miss one if you're not paying attention).

17. If you want to say hello to everyone, do it fast. You've got about 7.5 seconds per person. You'd better be able to qualify fast. BUT (and this is a big but), when a person seems to be a good prospect, spend a little extra time building some rapport for the follow-up. Don't waste time doing nonproductive things. Every second is important. If you have two days and 5,000 people are there – you get my point.

18. Don't prejudge anybody. You never know what boss may decide to come in casual clothing or wear someone else's badge so that he won't be bugged.

19. Read badges fast. Stay alert for your target badges (prospects you have selected, customers you've never met, types of businesses likely to need you) in the booth, in the aisles, while eating.

20. Be brief. Your remarks (other than questions) should be no more than 60 seconds.

21. Be to the point. Say something that tells prospects exactly what you do in terms of their needs.

22. Have fun and be funny. Enthusiasm and humor are contagious. People like to do business with winners, not whiners.

23. Shake firmly. Your handshake reflects your attitude. No one wants to shake hands with a dead fish.

24. Fight the urge to talk with fellow employees and friends. It's a disadvantage to both of you and a huge waste of time.

25. Establish buyer need. How can you sell anyone anywhere if you don't know what they need?

26. Get the information you need by probing first. Don't say too much too soon. Ask power and follow up questions that generate information, establish interest, determine need, and allow you to give your information in a meaningful way. Ask your best questions and have your most concise message ready to deliver when the timing is right. Before you deliver your problem-solving capabilities, know enough about the other person so that your information has impact. Know when to say what.

27. Show (tell) how you solve problems. He is bored to know what you do, unless you tell him in a way that serves him, or you have something the prospect thinks he needs. The prospect doesn't care what you do, unless what you do helps him.

28. Determine level of interest. If they need what you sell, how hot do they seem to buy? Note their interest level on their business card.

29. Pin the prospect down to the next action. Don't let a good prospect go without some agreement of what's next.

30. Write notes on the back of business cards immediately. If you make a lot of contacts, you'll never remember everything. Write information on the back of them as you speak and immediately after they depart. If you get 250 cards and have no notes on the back of them to follow up after the show, your effectiveness is reduced by 50% or more. (Use prospects' business cards as sales tools.) You can even write tentative appointment times on the backs of both yours and hers, to be confirmed after the show. Be sure to write down the personal (rapport) items – golf, children, sports, theater – to reference later when following up.

31. Be remembered. Say, give, or do something that will stay in the prospect's mind (in a positive, creative way).

32. Time's up. When you have delivered your message, made your contact, and secured the next meeting or action, move on.

33. Have a memorable handout or ad specialty. Something that will create long-term goodwill with your customer and prospect. Something to talk about when you follow up after the event.

34. Regroup at night and plan or replan for the next day. Things happen fast at a convention. You meet new people, deals are in the offing, and influential people in your industry are accessible. The only way to achieve the maximum benefit is to have a written game plan to start, and be flexible to change it as events unfold.

35. Stay sober all the time. It's a distinct advantage. If you get drunk and make an ass of yourself, you could do irreparable harm. Party, but party smart.

35.5 Have a great time! Don't press or be pressured; it will show. Trade shows are like life: The better attitude you have, the more successful you'll be.

Maximize your base of contacts and leads. Get the list of attendees from the association host after the show. This list will be useful to add to your database, to use for follow-up, and to contact the people you missed.

"**Conventions,
trade shows,
and business fairs
are the best contact
opportunity
and the most fun
a salesperson
can have –
with the right
preparation, focus,
and effort.**"

— Jeffrey Gitomer

THE SALES BIBLE

Part 9
Networking.
Success by Association(s)

The Book of Networking

We've got to start meeting like this.

Networking...

Your mother said, "Don't talk to strangers."

I've got nothing against motherhood, but if you want to succeed at networking, you'd better start talking to strangers.

How do you place a value on a solid, well-established business connection, a friend who is in a position to help you and your business?

These connections make careers.

You can never have too many friends.

So, how do you capture this opportunity? You network.

Just say, "Hello."

9.1

"A wise man knows everything,
a shrewd man knows everyone."
– Chinese proverb from a fortune cookie

Networking – the challenge of making success contacts.

How are you using networking to help build your career?
Make a networking plan. Today.

How many hours a week do you spend networking?
To get ahead it must be at least five (nonbusiness) hours a week.

How many of those hours are spent at optimum productivity?
It's easy to measure – you should get 20 new contacts per week.

This is your career. Your opportunity. Will you take advantage of the power of networking? If not now, when? You're working anyway. You may as well have some fun.

- **Networking is getting known by those who can help build your business.**

- **Networking is creating momentum toward business and career success.**

- **Networking is getting together with business contacts and turning them into customers and friends.**

- **Networking is building and nurturing long-term relationships.**

- **Networking is building a people resource bank that pays interest and dividends that compound annually for as long as you're alive.**

SECRET: Networking only works if you have a positive attitude.

Your goal is to successfully combine effective networking skills with a five-year networking plan of involvement, the results of which will achieve your objectives of:

- **More business contacts.**
- **More sales.**
- **More business education.**
- **More community involvement.**

Networker's Credo…
*I know if I get involved,
budget my time, attend regularly,
network my butt off, and do it right,
the results will exceed my expectations
of joining any organization.*

To succeed at networking, you must make a plan. Here's a questionnaire to help you formulate a game plan – use it!

- **Where do I network now?**
- **Where should I network?**
- **Where do my best customers network?**
- **What are three organizations I should investigate and possibly join?**
- **How many hours a week should I network?**
- **Who are five prime people I want to meet?**
- **What are my first-year networking goals?**
- **Do I have the networking skills I need?**
- **Do I have networking tools?**
- **Who is great at networking so that I can call and get help?**

Answer the questions above. They will help direct you toward a perfect networking game plan. The only thing missing from the plan is your commitment. Only you can supply that.

*If you attend a business networking event
with a friend or associate, split up!
It's a waste of time to walk,
talk, or sit together.*

Networking 101.
How to work a room.
The Fundamentals of Networking Success

Networking has become a vital business tool.

It's inexpensive (often free), time-effective/productive (you can usually make 20 to 30 contacts in a couple of hours), and has more of a social overtone (it's easier to do business socially – and it's fun).

If you question the value of networking, consider this: If there are 100 people in a room and you have two hours to network, you can speak to at least 50% of them and probably make 30 contacts. How long would it take you to make 50 sales calls in any other environment? Probably a week.

Many salespeople go to networking events – very few know how to network effectively. Here are 13.5 fundamental rules (tools) of networking that you can use to become a more effective and productive networker:

1. Preplan the event. Figure out who will be there, what you need to bring, what your objectives are, and if anyone else from your company should attend.

2. Show up early, ready to move, looking professional, full of cards.

3. Walk the crowd at least twice. Get familiar with the people and the room.

4. Target your prospects. Get a feel for who you'd like to meet.

5. Have your 30-second personal commercial down pat.

6. Keep your commercial to 30 seconds OR LESS.

7. Be happy, enthusiastic, and positive. Don't be grumbling or lamenting your tough day. People want to do business with a winner, not a whiner.

8. Say the other person's name at least twice. First to help you remember it, second because it's the most pleasing word to their ears.

9. Don't waste time if the person isn't a good prospect. But be polite when making your exit.

10. Eat early. It's hard to eat and mingle. Get your fill when you first arrive so that you are free to shake hands, talk without spitting food, and work the crowd effectively.

11. Don't drink. If everyone else is a bit loose, you'll have a distinct advantage by being sober. (Have a few beers afterward to celebrate all your new contacts.)

12. Don't smoke or smell like a cigarette.

13. Stay until the end. The longer you stay, the more contacts you'll make.

13.5 IMPORTANT NOTE … Have fun and be funny. It's not a brain cancer operation; it's a great time to get to know others and establish valuable relationships. **People like to be with people who are happy.**

If you say, "I go to networking events, but I don't get many prospects," it means you're not following the fundamentals, OR you're not networking where your prime prospects might be.

WHERE TO GO: Event selection is as important as networking itself. Ask your top five customers where they go for their monthly meetings. Start going there.

Each week, your local business journal and the business section of your daily paper publish a list of business events. The chamber of commerce publishes a monthly calendar. Don't overlook social and cultural events as networking possibilities. Select the events that may attract your prospects or people you want to get to know.

To make the most of a networking event,
spend 75% of your time
with people you don't know.

Networking 102.
How to milk a room.
The Secrets of Networking Success

"I wish I could get more leads when I network." If you have said this to yourself more than once, and you're willing to get serious about the science of networking, I have listed some ideas and strategies that will help you succeed in getting solid prospects.

If you're not following the fundamental rules of networking (see the previous section), don't even try the subtle ones – they won't work.

Here are the 10.5 subtleties of networking success:

1. Early in the event and near the end of the event, stand by the entrance if possible. At the start you can see everyone and establish your targets, and at the end you can catch anyone you missed.

2. Spend 75% of your time with people you don't know. Hanging around with fellow employees and friends is fun but won't put any prospect cards in your pocket or make any valuable contacts.

3. Spend 25% of your time building existing relationships. Talk to your customers. The better you get to know them, the stronger their loyalty to you and your company.

4. Don't give your information out too soon. After you give your 5-10 second introduction, ask the other person what they do *before you start talking in depth about what you do.*

5. After your prospect has told you about himself, your next move is a choice between establishing rapport (finding common interests) and an opportunity to arouse interest in your product/service. What the prospect said in his introduction will be your guide.

6. If the person seems to be a good prospect, you must establish some common ground besides business if you want to ensure an easier path to doing business. Find one thing you both like or know about.

7. Try to appoint the prospect now. If you want to get the prospect's card, offer your card first, or give a reason you need the card ("Give me your card and I'll mail you some information"). If the prospect is reluctant to give you a card, he/she is likely to be hard to appoint later.

8. Write all pertinent info on the back of the prospect's card immediately. You will need this to refer to when following up.

9. Don't sell your product/service. Just establish some rapport, some confidence, and *sell an appointment.*

10. Be aware of time. After you have established the contact, gotten the business card, established rapport, and confirmed your next action (mail, call, appointment), move on to the next prospect.

10.5 Play a game with a co-worker. If you go with someone from your company, bet who gets more (qualified) cards. The more you bet, the less likely you'll spend a second together.

Now that you've got the fundamentals down, let's capitalize on your new knowledge. Networking is a powerful, cost-effective marketing weapon. If utilized properly, it can provide the basis for your business growth. It did for me.

To facilitate implementing your networking plan, you need a few more guidelines. Here are my 9.5 personal networking secret rules for success:

1. I follow the 50-butt rule. If there are more than 50 butts in one room, my butt is there too.

2. Learn how to make small talk important talk. Be brief and to the point. If someone asks what you do, say it quickly and succinctly.

3. Don't flap your gums just to be talking. When you engage your mouth, make it count.

4. Know the kinds of problems you can solve rather than a bunch of boring facts about your product or service. Talk in terms of how you solve problems rather than the product or service you offer.

5. Avoid negatives at all cost. Don't complain or speak poorly about a person or business. You never know if the prospect you're talking to has some connection, interest, or affiliation with the people, company, or product you're slamming.

6. Be polite. *Please* and *thanks* go a long way toward creating an impression, whether they are present or absent.

7. Don't spend too much time with one person or you defeat the purpose of networking. If you find a good connection or lead, spend a LITTLE extra time. Know when you've said and heard enough. Be smart enough to make an appointment, pique interest, and MOVE ON.

8. Your objective is to take advantage of the entire room. If you spend three minutes with a prospect, that gives you a possibility of 20 contacts per hour. Every second is valuable. The size of the event dictates the amount of time you should spend with each person. The larger the event, the shorter time per contact, and the less time you should spend with people you know.

9. Get involved in the organizations where you network. People identify with and do business with leaders.

9.5 Remember, at a networking event everyone wants to sell! You may have to play a *buyer* in order to get a chance to be a *seller*. You must be able to wear either hat. Learning the skills of networking will provide you the opportunity to be either … and in complete control of the situation.

"Today I called up all of my business associates and told them what a bunch of idiots they are. It's called networking."

If you are able to establish rapport when networking,
you will have a perfect conversation starter
when you follow-up to make an appointment.

Establishing rapport
when working a room.

Webster's dictionary defines *rapport* with several words: relation, connection, accord, harmony, and agreement.

Rapport is a subtle yet vital aspect of the selling process.

Establishing rapport with a prospect at a networking event enhances your ability to appoint (and sell) in the ensuing follow-up.

Here are some guidelines to maximize your productivity at (and after) a networking event:

WHEN YOU ALREADY KNOW THE PERSON. If you have a business agenda, discuss it within two minutes. If the person is your customer, spend a couple minutes building the personal relationship by establishing mutual interests. If he or she is talking to someone you don't know, get introduced and see if there's a fit. If you make a promise or commitment, get another card from the person and *immediately* write it down on the back. No matter what, after five minutes move on.

WHEN YOU DON'T KNOW THE PERSON. Get information before you give your 30-second personal commercial. Don't elaborate or try to sell until the other person has talked about themselves and you have tried to establish mutual interest. Ask an open-ended question about how they now use your type of product or service. A question that will engage the prospect, make them talk about themselves, and make them begin to open up and reveal. As soon as they broach a personal issue, grab it and expand on it.

When you engage a prospect, try to find out his personal interests. After the traditional exchange of business information, try to find out what the prospect does after work, or what he's doing next weekend. You might even try out a couple of interest items if an event is near or just passed, like a ball game, car race, concert, play, or business function.

After you have gotten to know a little about this person, you can begin the "let's get together later to finish this discussion" part that will solidify the all-important appointment.

During my networking years in Charlotte (before I was on the road 250 days per year), I spent 60 hours a month meeting other people and making connections that led to sales. Not just leads groups and business groups; I was also involved with four community and civic organizations.

I regularly attended meetings, gave my time to make the groups better, always tried for leadership positions, and worked hard to establish and maintain relationships.

I spent my first ten years in Charlotte building my network. My findings can be summed up in two words. It works!

How and where do you network? Do you just attend functions or are you active in the group?

Are you just a taker, or are you willing to get involved and help the group succeed with your hard work and dedication?

Here are 14.5 guidelines for joining a networking organization and succeeding at networking your way to rich relationships:

1. Go where your prospects are. Try to select groups and organizations that have the best chance of bearing fruit. One good indication is if one or some of your present customers belong.

2. When you join an organization, don't wait for your welcome kit to arrive. The kit won't contain any success formula. You create that on your own. To identify your best resource for networking success, just look in the mirror the next chance you get. (Pretty good looking, huh?)

3. To benefit, you must commit to be involved, then get involved.

4. It takes time to build trust and get to understanding. For the first few meetings, just listen and observe. Pushing too quickly gives others a wary feeling. See where and how you can best fit into the group. Just get to know and help quality people. The rest will take care of itself.

5. When you commit, be there consistently and perform. By attending regularly, you will be seen and known as consistent.

6. A 5-year game plan is essential. *Ask yourself:*
- **Where do my prospects/customers participate?**
- **Who do I want to develop relationships with?**
- **What are my expected results?**
- **How much time must I commit?**
- **Who are the important people involved that I must contact?**
- **Who else from my company should be involved?**

7. Give first. This is a key to any relationship, not just business. The classic Zig Ziglar line, *"You can get whatever you want if you help enough people get whatever they want,"* is the best way to describe "give first."

8. Don't measure. If you count who owes who what favor, forget it. Just get to know and help quality people. The rest will take care of itself. (Are you getting the idea?)

9. Don't push. If you are sincere about establishing long-term relationships, don't put pressure on someone to deliver immediate business. I'm not saying don't do business if the opportunity presents itself. I am saying don't push business.

10. Be prepared when you get there. Have the tools (both physical and mental) to make contacts. Your business card is only valuable if your ability to engage (with your personal commercial) has been mastered.

11. After you meet a prospect in a group, get one-on-one. You can get to know someone quite well in an hour if you talk about real issues and avoid weather and politics.

12. Every networking contact need not be a sale. Often one breeds the other. Get to know and help quality people. The rest will take care of itself.

13. Be seen (get known) as a leader. By getting involved, you will be observed by your prospect. He or she will get to know you as a performer, a doer, and a leader.

14. People will do business with you once they get to know you and see you perform. Your customers and prospects are here! All you have to do is identify them and work (network) with them side by side.

14.5 Mature relationships breed sales. If you build a solid relationship with someone, he will go out of his way to find you business. And the recurring universal networking rule applies here too: *Just get to know and help quality people. The rest will take care of itself.*

*An easy way to see how
your network is growing.*

The Official
Networking Game.

When you go to a sporting event, concert, mall, flea market, restaurant, or you're traveling – you can play The Official Networking Game.

The object of the game is to know more people than the person you're with.

Here are the rules of the game. You get:

> **1 POINT** if you know someone.
>
> **2 POINTS** if the person sees you (and acknowledges you) first.
>
> **3 POINTS** if you see a minor celebrity (sports figure, DJ).
>
> **5 POINTS** if you kiss someone of the opposite sex.
>
> **5 POINTS** if a celebrity acknowledges you first.

IT'S BEST TO AGREE ON WHEN THE GAME STARTS AND ENDS: For example, at a basketball game, it starts as you enter the rotunda at halftime. You walk around once and return to your section and the game is over.

There are two words
that are music to my ears
when playing the networking game.
"Hey, Gitomer!"

"Your ability to build
a successful network is
tied to your determination
and dedication to take
whatever time is
necessary
to build quality
relationships.
And you're lucky –
the outcome
of your success is totally
self-determined."

– *Jeffrey Gitomer*

The Book
of Trends

What's New?

Trends...

Read about people
who are taking
the personal responsibility
for going the extra mile
for their customers,
for their company,
and for themselves.

Take what you learn, and
start a trend of your own.

Here's how...

10.1

The new breed of salespeople...
they rely on truth
and product knowledge,
with a minor in sales skills.

The new breed of salesperson.
A non-salesperson.

Jeff Chadwick is a new breed of salesman – or should I say non-salesman. For years he worked for Classic Graphics, one of Charlotte's premier printers. Chadwick was in production, and he had about reached the top of his earnings potential at the plant position he was in. He gave all the shop tours. He loved it. People would say, "He's the best salesman you've got." One day Chadwick sold a surplus printing press. His boss, Bill Gardner, told him he should go into sales. So Chadwick decided to go into sales. Commission sales.

"If you ask me what the alternative-of-choice close or the sharp-angle close is, I don't have a clue," Chadwick says. "But if you ask me can you gatefold (double fold) this piece of paper, I can sure tell you that – and that's what the customer wants to know. I love sales. It's a lot of work. Fast paced – no one who needs printing ever says, 'Take your time.' Everyone needs it yesterday."

I asked Chadwick to define his sales assets and attributes. "Enthusiasm. Persistence. Pride. Personal pride. I have Classic Graphics posters on my walls at home. I love being around my peers so I can tell them who I work for," he said. "I find my best sales asset is my ability to help the customer select things that will work. I rely heavily on my product knowledge."

Product knowledge is also the sales foundation for Clarkson Jones. The company he works for, Carolina Asphalt, is a firm specializing in quality parking lot repair and maintenance. Jones spent seven years supervising jobs and heavy equipment operation.

During that time he gained incredible product knowledge. He began developing great relationships with customers because he had the ability to solve problems and he always gave straight answers (a characteristic shared by 99% of the new breed).

A few years ago, Jones realized that people were calling him to place orders rather than going through the company's salespeople. Why? "I guess I was nonthreatening to them," Jones said. "I was the guy who got the job done, gave great service, and knew how to solve their problems. Customers just naturally gravitated to me." Life as a salesperson is different for Jones. "I don't miss my old day-to-day grind in the field," he said. "But I could not be in the position I am today without that hands-on experience."

Last year was a banner year for Carolina Asphalt. This year Jones's personal sales are on track to exceed the sales of the company's best salesman.

There are thousands of salespeople like Chadwick and Jones that are beginning to emerge. Here are some of the characteristics that are prevalent in the new breed:

- **Non-manipulative selling at its purest.** They get to the sale by being truthful.

- **Nonthreatening.** They are not perceived as salespeople; therefore, the customer isn't as on-guard.

- **Helpful.** They are not pushy.

- **Consultative.** They can make meaningful recommendations and suggestions based on knowledge of what actually works from their personal experience.

- **Total product knowledge.** They have the information a customer needs to make an informed decision or solve a problem.

- **Error prevention.** Their experience can spot a POTENTIAL error and prevent it.

- **On top of the job.** The job goes smoother because they start it right and are on top of it all the way – just like they were in the shop.

Do you work in the office or factory and wonder if sales is for you?
If you answer *yes* to these questions, report to your sales manager in
the morning:

- **Do you have great technical or product knowledge?**
- **Have you hit the pay ceiling?**
- **Do you get along well with customers or have good people skills?**

If you think you can do it, you are probably right. But you must be willing
to take risks.

And, hey, salesperson without hands-on inside experience – Get some!
Devote some time to working in every area of your business. Your inside
team will respect you more, you will have a better understanding of
your product and co-workers, and your customers will benefit from your
newfound product knowledge. So will your wallet.

*"Welcome to my motivational seminar. If you are here tonight
instead of home on your sofa, then you're already a motivated person
and don't need me! Good night and thank you for coming."*

*"I learn how to win
by networking and developing
relationships with winners."*
– Bob Salvin

What's Bob Salvin
got to do with it? Lots!

"You don't take a chance when you bet on yourself," says Bob Salvin, an international distributor of medical products adapted for implant dentistry. He has customers in all 50 states and in 27 countries. How does he get them?

"I think of myself as humbly assertive. I give first. If I start to think what I'll get back or start to count my orders before I get them, I always lose. My philosophy is to give as much as I can. Eventually it comes back much greater than the original gift, and from the most unexpected places."

Bob's definition of marketing is getting "your telephone to ring with qualified buyers." And here's how he does it:

- **Giving out thousands of catalogs to the right people at a trade show.**
- **Mailing catalogs after a trade show.**
- **Mailing the catalog to qualified lists.**
- **Mailing catalogs to preregistered meeting lists – buyers put him on their list of 'Must Visit.'**
- **Mailing quantities of catalogs to dentists.**
- **Offering clinical courses in their offices.**
- **Asking lecturing doctors to recommend him.**
- **Talking to a qualified customer at a meeting or trade show.**

"I have developed a 'cross-mentoring' network locally, nationally, and internationally. I talk to other people who do part of what I do and try to help them as they help me. Sometimes I call them – sometimes they call me. Not direct competitors, but businesses who have the same marketing components. I talk to others who do catalogs and trade shows, and those who run distribution centers. I learn from them. They learn from me."

"I learn how to win by networking and developing relationships with winners."

"We do a tremendous amount of direct mail and tradeshow marketing. I know that to be successful, I have to capitalize on these leads. I also know that to turn those leads into sales, I'd better be extraordinary."

"People love to buy," says Salvin, "but customers tend to buy from people they know and trust. Every dentist has a closet full of stuff he thought he would like, or thought he would need but didn't. My objective is to never have any Salvin products in that closet. A doctor's time is short. I've got to get their attention fast and gain interest so I can gain more time."

Here are a few more gems from Bob:

• **I DON'T SELL. I MAKE IT EASY TO BUY.** Prospects and customers get multiple personal exposures – and toll-free communication.

• **I PROVIDE MULTIPLE CHOICES AT MULTIPLE LEVELS.** All kinds of options with every product we sell: technical literature, technical literature plus a video demonstrating the product, or literature, the video, and a 30-day trial.

• **I MAKE IT EASY TO DECIDE.** Evaluate at your leisure. Test it in your environment for three weeks.

• **I MAKE IT EASY TO RETURN.** But very few choose that option.

• **I'M A PUPPY DOG MARKETER.** "I offer highly technical products on 30-day trials. Less than 1 in 30 return these products. But that's a misleading figure. Our referrals from those who keep the products far exceed the number of products returned. We have added video training to enhance the sales ratio."

• **I CREATE MULTIPLE WAYS TO WIN.** "I create different benefits, terms, and perceived values. The comfort level of my prospect is paramount to their deciding to buy."

• **I CREATE ENOUGH CONFIDENCE TO MAKE THE SALE.** Then deliver in a manner that creates long-term opportunities. "I explore how many ways I can develop communications so that the customer gets my message in a way that he or she finds comfortable."

Bob Salvin doesn't always have the lowest price. And he's proud of it. He tells a customer, "First let me tell you the price, but price is not why most of my customers (94% of whom are return customers) buy. They buy the value, the extended warranty, the extended terms, the help to finance, and the technical support. They buy the product, the support, and the organization – they buy the price." WOW!

"It's not what it costs. It's what it produces."

"I make sales in the most unorthodox ways I've ever seen," Salvin says. "I'll invite a prospect 1,000 miles away to have lunch with me." I say, "Let's have lunch together at our desks, over the phone. I send my product ($1,000 to $5,000 value), we discuss the possibilities, and I do a demo over the phone while we eat a sandwich. The products we sell are idea sensitive, and a big part of our value is to convey proper use."

How many ways do you have for your customers to buy or get to know about and buy your product? *Here are 10 more of Salvin's multiple ways to win:*

1. Literature and technical manuals.
2. Training video.
3. Third-party referral.
4. Extended warranty (beyond factory).
5. Lifetime warranty.
6. Return it if not satisfied.
7. Training.
8. Support before and after the sale.
9. Sample of product or free trial.
10. Loaned equipment during repair.

"By eliminating ways to fail, you give the prospect comfort to buy, and buy now. In my marketing plan I have ostensibly eliminated the risk of my prospect making a poor choice."

Bob Salvin is not just smart, he's wise. Here are a few more of his philosophies of marketing that you can benefit from:

1. Try to personalize everything you do.
2. Look for ways to go beyond what's expected, then do them without being asked.
3. Make prospects or customers think about you, even if they don't buy.
4. Make your prospect feel comfortable enough to do business with you.
5. Make them laugh.
6. Make the prospect excited to get your stuff.
7. Learn what is important to them.
8. Give prospects choices they can't refuse.
9. Create new ways to say, "Thank you for your business."

"By eliminating ways to fail, you give the prospect comfort to buy, and buy now. In my marketing plan I have ostensibly eliminated the risk of my prospect making a poor choice."

"I'm Southern polite when I sell. I ask permission to do everything," says Salvin. I ask, "Is that okay?" Evidently it is, because Salvin's phone rings off the hook.

2008 UPDATE:
Salvin Dental and Bob Salvin – fast forward 15 years. Still setting the standard. Still easy to do business with. Still walking their talk and banking their hard earned profits.

Bob is still at the helm, but has several excellent, dedicated people running strategic parts of his business. All with the attitude of "sell and serve."

To differentiate their sales team in a very competitive market, they hire the "green beret, rather than the infantry," educate them with entrepreneurial business skills, and empower them to deal with their customers on a decision-maker-to-decision-maker basis rather then merely play the role of salesperson.

Salvin Dental hires only proven performers showing great attitude, energy, and "sparkle" in their personalities. Members of Salvin's sales team will likely be proven performers with President's Club histories and perfect references. To get good references, Salvin calls former employers, hoping to get their voicemail, and leaves a message asking for a call back if the individual would be a "stellar candidate" for this opportunity.

Their goal is to develop and retain top performers. The company uses a "smokeless, mirrorless" sales compensation plan, and benchmarks each new salesperson against their proven performers to identify and provide reading and training on the areas that need improvement.

They train their sales team by having them take the same surgical courses as the doctors do. Salvin's company does 240 hands-on surgical courses and trade shows per year with the objective of putting their sales team in front of groups of qualified buyers.

In their business, great service creates the ultimate long-term sales opportunity. Every part of their internal customer care process is focused on allowing their customers to order as late as 4:59PM and still get their order out the same day.

Salvin believes in education so that he can have the best trained sales force in the industry. The company's surgical product line has over 900 items in it and they don't want to put an unqualified salesperson in front of a very qualified customer.

Salvin's business model and dedication to service has enabled him to partner with world-renowned thought leaders and this partnership serves for the betterment of the industry.

Bob insists that his customers are treated more than fairly in every transaction and at every contact.

Bob does not believe in voicemail or automated attendants. They don't ever waste their customer's time going through a receptionist or call screener.

Every customer call is answered, before the third ring, by a live empowered person. On the fourth ring, customer calls go directly to, and are answered by the CEO, the President, or the National Sales Manager. WOW!

SALVIN DENTAL HAS A GREAT WEBSITE WITH HIGH PLACEMENT ON THE MAJOR SEARCH ENGINES. Their goal is to ensure that the doctor has the right stuff to get the best result for his patients. Customers can shop by keyword or by surgical procedure, and many will call their sales team who will guide them through the steps of a surgical procedure as they look at the website together.

THEY HAVE TESTIMONIALS AND PHOTOS IN THEIR CATALOG FROM MANY OF THE MOST RESPECTED DOCTORS IN THEIR INDUSTRY. These are all unpaid endorsements, and unlike many companies who put testimonials at the end of a proposal, they put testimonials at the front of their catalog so that any new customer will immediately see that he is in great company by choosing to do business with Salvin Dental.

Bob and his leadership team spend more than 20% of their time developing their people from a sales and business prospective including sharing all numbers so everyone has a better understanding of the business, not just their job.

THEIR GOAL IS TO BE A CLASS ACT IN ALL THAT THEY DO. And they have been achieving their goal for 20 years.

THIS IS NOT A COMMERCIAL FOR SALVIN DENTAL. 99.9% of you will never need what Salvin sells. I'm presenting this model as one that you can copy for your business. Everyone wants to develop a sales culture – Salvin has done it. Everyone wants to develop a service culture – Salvin has done it. Everyone wants to make it easy to business with their company – Salvin has done it.

Get the message.
Take the lesson.
Emulate the Salvin Success Strategy.

The Book of Numbers

Up Your Income!

Numbers don't lie...
and they don't make
excuses.

Do you?

If you don't hit your
numbers in sales, you're
only doing a number on
yourself.

The law of numbers is the
law of averages combined
with your ability to master
the science of selling, help
other people, and establish
long-term relationships.

You got into sales because
it had unlimited income
potential.

Are you limiting yourself
because you failed to
commit to the dedication
necessary to achieve
"unlimited"?

Unlimit yourself!

11.1

Selling success is a numbers game.
And a magic game.
You must combine the magic
with your numbers to produce.

The pipeline of success.

I am about to present you with a formula and a challenge.

If you're looking for a magic formula, go read a book on the life and times of Houdini.

If you're looking for magic, that's different. You have all the magic needed to double your present income. All you have to do is learn and execute the tricks.

Here is the theory behind the formula. These questions will provide the answers to your sales earning capacity:

- **How many sales do you want to make per day, per month?**
- **What is the dollar value of your average sale?**
- **To make your goal, how many dollars in sales do you have to make per day, per month?**
- **How many prospects do you need to see to make a sale?**
- **What is the set of numbers I need to get to these answers?**

Want to do it in 30 days? Easy – up your urgency. Get committed. I can supply the jet plane. It's up to you to provide the jet fuel. When I started out in sales, I used to pick up the paper and read the obituaries until I found someone who was close to my age. It lit a candle under me for weeks.

Here are the 12.5 elements in the formula…

1. Your attitude. The key to your success. Get CDs now. Listen two hours a day for six months. Stop doing or listening to negative things.

2. Your goals. Set them today. Read the seven steps in the *Post-it Note* section again. Use the Post-it Notes beginning right now.

3. Your networking. Find out where your best customers and prospects meet (trade association, chamber, club). Begin attending every meeting you can. It is imperative that you attend regularly.

4. Your power questions. Write 'em. Learn 'em. Use 'em.

5. Your power statements. Write 'em. Learn 'em. Use 'em.

6. Your sales tools. Figure out what tools you need and get 'em.

7. Your sales knowledge. Get CDs and listen to them. Alternate with the attitude CDs. Use the idea as soon as you hear it. Read every chapter in this book twice. One chapter per day.

8. Your preparedness. Are you truly ready to sell? If you are, you will. If you're not, you won't. The opposite of preparedness is failure.

9. Your follow-up. Tenacious, creative persistence that leads to a sale.

10. Your sales numbers. Making yourself see the numbers you need to build your pipeline and keep it full. Find your formula and use it.

11. Your prospect pipeline. Seeing the proper number of people a day who are qualified to buy builds your pipeline. The key to double income is having the right number of prospects ready to buy.

12. Your commitment. Write it to yourself. Tell others who will help you. Your commitment is your personal promise to yourself. Keep it at all costs.

12.5 Your self-discipline. Your determination and ability to achieve your goals and live up to your commitments.

There is a sales adage that says, "Your chances for success increase in proportion to the number of sales calls you make." It's amazing how the truth can be so simple. *If it's so simple, why don't you do it?*

Good fundamental sales skills and solid product knowledge are meaningless unless you see and follow up the proper number of prospects.

Seeing the numbers creates a pipeline…the number of prospects at or near the buying point.

A quick check of your numbers will reveal why your sales are booming or slumping…

If you appoint and present to 10 prospects, two will buy no matter what you do and two won't buy no matter what you do. The other six are on the fence and will buy or not buy as a result of what you say or don't say. A sale will be made either way. Either you sell them on yes, or they sell you on no.

Your follow-up habits and skills are responsible for 80% of your sales.

It boils down to your self-discipline. How good is it? How consistent is it? Without it you should consider an assembly-line job, because you won't make it in sales. Here is a sample formula to keep your sales pipeline (and wallet) full:

1. Make 10 new prospect calls per day.
2. Make 10 new appointments per week, preferably by Monday.
3. Make 10 follow-up calls per day.
4. Make one strong presentation in the morning and one in the afternoon.
5. Take prospects or customers to lunch four times a week.
6. Join two business or leads associations.
7. Attend at least two networking functions per week (where your best customers or prospects go).
8. Keep accurate daily records.

If you don't record what you do each day, your ability to follow up is nil. Your daily sales log (or computerized sales records) should keep and total the following statistics:

- **Calls out by type (new, follow-up)**
- **Number of follow-ups made today**
- **New appointments made today**
- **Appointments seen today**
- **Sales made today**
- **Dollars contracted for today**
- **Dollars collected today**
- **Commissions/dollars earned today**

IMPORTANT NOTE: Keep separate sheets or files for each contact. Your reporting should be by contact status, not by time status (what you did on Tuesday morning). If your manager is still in the Dark Ages about contact management or has that paranoia of needing to know where you are every minute of the day, ask him to read *The Book of Leadership* in this volume.

Your contact management program will tell you where you are in the selling cycle.

Answer these questions – they reveal the truth about your potential for sales success:

- **Do you have a hot prospect list daily?**
- **Are you doing (and recording) the numbers it takes to make your sales goals a reality?**
- **Is your sales pipeline (prospects you can convert to sales) full?**
- **How many prospects are you working on? (Should be 100+.)**
- **Are you working on enough prospects to fill your sales goals for the next month? If not, your pipeline isn't full, is it? Go back to the 12.5 elements listed above. They hold the key to your sales backlog (and your success).**

You know what to do. Why don't you do it? Here are some reasons why you don't (the answers are provided in parentheses):

- **You're on your own and don't know how to do it.** (Poor training. Get some good training soon.)
- **You're lazy.** (Find new employment.)
- **You have poor work habits.** (You can change them with 30 days of doing it differently.)
- **Bad boss.** (Don't blame failure on others. This is no reason to fail if you are determined enough to succeed.)
- **No or ineffective reporting system.** (Get a laptop, or make a form and do it yourself.)
- **Low, poor, or unfair compensation package.** (Change jobs.)

If you see and call enough prospects per day, per week, per month… you will build your pipeline. A full pipeline will bring you sales you never imagined.

Do you floss every day? You know you should, but you don't. Eventually all your teeth will fall out, but you can't see them eroding day by day until it's too late.

FLOSS EVERY DAY – YOUR TEETH WILL BE PERFECT. The same is true about the fundamentals of sales follow-up. If you don't follow up every day, your sales backlog will rot.

ADD TO YOUR PIPELINE EVERY DAY AND DO YOUR FOLLOW-UPS – YOUR SALES WILL BE PERFECT.

Want proof? Go back to the best week you ever had and look at the numbers that made it happen. I guarantee if you work those numbers every week, your sales (and earnings) will soar.

All it takes is self-determination and hard work.That's the magic.
Ask any magician.

The
Book of
Exodus

12.1

Let my money go.

Exodus was the road to freedom.

The end of *The Sales Bible* is really the beginning. The beginning of a revolution in your sales career.

It's a Sales Crusade, and you are your own Sales Crusader.

You're on a journey to personal sales success.

Others won't do it for you, but others will help you, if you help them first.

You have the opportunity to take the wealth of information you've gotten from this book and turn it into a fortune.

I hope you do.

Dads teach sales success without knowing it.

My dad set examples for me like yours did for you. Sometimes they were good examples; sometimes they were bad. But every time my dad set one, I paid attention to it, and decided when I grew up whether I would follow that example.

Here are a few of his ideas to ponder:

DON'T LET LAWYERS OR GREED SWAY GOOD BUSINESS JUDGMENT. In 1960, after 15 successful years of operation, my dad's factory burned to the ground. We were stunned. Two days later, the insurance adjuster came to our house with a check for $750,000 to settle the fire loss and let my dad rebuild his business. My dad's lawyer took him aside and told him he thought we could get a million and to reject the offer. My dad went for the million. Three years later, my dad settled for $333,000, one-third of which went to the lawyer. The lessons I learned were: Lawyers are for legal advice, not business advice; and take your losses quickly and move on to rebuild your life. Those lessons helped me when I faced failure.

PROVIDE SIMPLE SOLUTIONS. One night my brother turned over in his single bed and fell onto the floor. He went downstairs and pounded on my parents' door. "Dad, I fell out of bed!" he moaned. "Get back in, son," my father said.

Often the most simple solutions to problems are the best. But they're hard to uncover if you're only concentrating on the problem.

ANYTHING 10 GRAND WON'T CURE? Coming home from college, I was sometimes in a bad mood. One day when I was slamming doors and looking glum, my dad asked, "Problems, son?" "A few," I muttered. "Anything 10 grand won't cure?" he asked. My whole mood changed. "No," I said. And realized I didn't really have any problems.

ANYTHING 10 GRAND WON'T CURE? Ask yourself that question the next time you're lamenting your woes. If 10 grand (or money) would solve the problem, you really don't have a problem.

"In the end...
There is only one point of view that matters.
There is only one perspective that matters.
There is only one perception that matters.
The customer's."

– Jeffrey Gitomer

Commit yourself!

For 40 years I have been on a personal crusade to be the best salesperson (and now sales trainer) in the world. I set that goal (in stone) the first time I ever realized there was a *science of selling* – that selling was a set of learnable, repeatable skills that I could modify to my style and personality. I knew that if I became the best, I could achieve anything I wanted. When I combined the science of selling with my attitude and sense of humor, I provided myself the gateway for tremendous achievement.

> When I combined the science of selling with my attitude and my sense of humor, I provided myself the gateway for tremendous achievement.

I wrote this book (and all my other books) to help guide you to the same achievement. Take 30 minutes and read something about *The Crusades*. They were much more than a religious war. *The Crusades* were about people *passionately* going after what they believed in. They did it regardless of the hardship and risk. Do you?

SALES IS NOT A RELIGION, BUT IT IS A WAY OF LIFE. It shouldn't consume your life. You can't worship the sale. Rather, it should be incorporated into your life. Naturally. what you sell has to feel good to YOU, before you can make it feel good for others. Being in sales enhances life and embraces the philosophy for living to its maximum potential.

Doubling your income isn't pie in the sky. If you are determined to get to the top, here are the principles that will get you there.

Here are 11.5 principles to lead your own sales crusade.

1. Get a positive attitude and keep it. Most everyone thinks they have a positive attitude, but they don't, Usually not even close. Earl Nightingale, in his legendary recording, *The Strangest Secret*, reveals the secret of a positive attitude: *We become what we think about* ... but it's a dedicated discipline that must be practiced every day. People don't understand that the essence of attitude is not a feeling – it's a state of mind that is self-induced.

You are in complete control of it. You determine what your attitude is. It has nothing to do with what happens to you. It's not about money or success. **It's the way you dedicate yourself to the way you think.** But you must rededicate yourself to the principles of it every day. How do you attain a positive attitude? Begin to surround yourself with positive ideas and positive people. Read and listen to positive writers and speakers. Believe you can achieve it. Don't listen to other people who tell you you're nuts – they're just jealous. Start now and work at it every day.

2. Set goals, and make a commitment to achieve them.

- **Project yourself** – If your targets are in front of you, it makes it easy to hit them. Being able to hit the targets depends on your focus. The clearer your focus, the more likely you are to hit a bullseye.

- **Commit yourself** – Which do you plan for more: your vacation or your life? If you don't emotionally, physically, mentally, and spiritually commit yourself to achievement, it is likely you will fall short.

- **Satisfy yourself** – Make a list of the benefits of achieving each goal and carry the list with you. Achieving a goal is incredibly self-satisfying. It gives you a feeling of accomplishment, purpose and the inspiration to set out and achieve the next goal. Big Clue … Figure out the daily dose. An amount you can measure, an amount you can achieve. Determine how much you need to do each day to reach your goal in short steps (pennies per day, ounces per day, pounds per week, calls per day, dollars per sale) and do that daily dose each day.

3. Dedicate yourself to mastering the science of selling. *Learn something new about sales or your attitude every day.* Feed your head with new knowledge that will help you make that next sale. If you want to become an expert in sales, learning one new idea per day gives you 220 new ideas per year. If you sell for five years, you'll have more than 1,000 ideas at your disposal. Amazing what you can do if you just do something small every day. If you just dedicate 15 to 30 minutes a day to learning something new about sales and achieving a positive attitude, at the end of five years you will be a master salesperson and have a great attitude about life.

4. Design a networking plan and implement it. Make a 5-year plan to get known and get to know those who can build your business. Networking is the fastest, surest method to increase your sales and stature.

5. Be a leader. Look for and strive for leadership positions. Take charge of a committee; speak to a civic group, write an article for a local paper. People love to do business with leaders.

6. Get involved in your community. Select a charity or community organization worthy of your time and make a contribution. You'll grow in success and reputation, but more important you'll feel great about living to help others.

7. Know your prospect and your prospect's business before you make the sales call. Get the information you need to make every appointment intelligent and impactful. Use this guideline to assure it: *Ask the buyer questions that only he or she knows the answers to.*

8. Be memorable in all that you do. Take a creative idea to each sales call. Have the courage to live your dreams and goals. Your work and dedication will inspire others. Your words will be remembered because you backed them up with deeds and delivery. Will they talk about you after you're gone?

9. Help other people. When you establish this belief as one of the foundations of your selling process, the attributes that accompany it are the keys to making your customer feel motivated to act and confident enough to buy. There is an offshoot of this philosophy: *Get business for others.* It is as powerful as any sales tool you can imagine.

10. Stay focused and look for opportunity. How important is it to be focused? In 1982, after a big imprinted sportswear show, I was at the Dallas airport when I noticed a guy I met from a T-shirt manufacturing company. He was swearing at the American Express money machine. It seems the machine ate his card. He was looking desperate. I walked over, reintroduced myself, found out the problem, and loaned him $100 so that he would have cash for the trip home. Two days later, he sent me a check for $100 and a thank-you note. Turns out he was the president of his company. Two months later, he called me and asked if I was interested in printing garments for the 1984 Olympics. He had the sublicense to manufacture from Levi's. We had a state-of-the-art printing facility. I said, "Of course." He gave me a contract to print every shirt – 1,600,000 garments, $750,000 worth of business – because I was paying attention at the airport. And because I was living my philosophy of "help other people."

11. Establish long-term relationships with everyone. If you look
to establish a long-term relationship each time you sell, it assures that the
integrity, sincerity, honesty, and doing what's best for the customer are
a given. Make long-term a prerequisite for selling. Be sure to share this
philosophy with your customers.

11.5 Have fun. Look at the most successful people in any field. One thing
they have in common is that they love what they do. They pursue what
they do with a passion and enthusiasm that is admirable (and contagious).
How much fun are you having?

*"I spent years on the Road to Success, but I was driving
in the wrong direction!"*

"I hope all your appointments are one-call closes that lead to long-term relationships."

– Jeffrey Gitomer

Afterword...
When I grow up.

I always wanted to be a businessman, an entrepreneur, like my dad.
I decided to commute to college so that I could be close to home and
his business.

My mother, Florence, passed away in 1986. My fondest memory is of her
chasing my car as I backed out of the driveway on my first day to register
for college (Temple University). "Take pre-med," she screamed. "You can
always switch." But I wanted to be a businessman, like my dad.

In college, I played Scrabble every day with my then best friend, Michael
Toll. He usually won. It taught me about words and how to use them.
Michael provided me with the challenge of winning at games, both sports
and intellectual. He'll tell you he was better than me at everything. I feel
the same about him. That was the fun. We rarely studied.

Six years later, I finally dropped out of college. I traveled in Europe for a
year (and came to the realization that I knew very little compared to what
there was to know, which is funny, because I left for Europe knowing
everything). I came home and started a business (manufacturing beanbag
chairs) and a family (twin girls in 1972).

One day, Jay Plasky and Barton Cohen (college friends) came to my
office and started talking to me about this money-making idea. It seems
they had been involved with this guy named Glenn Turner, and he had
an idea to get people to invest in an opportunity that was not quite clear
to me, but everyone was making money – big money – and they all had
these *positive attitudes*. After a few alterations, Jay, Barton, and I embarked
on a multilevel marketing deal (which was referred to in those days as a
pyramid scheme).

Every day, from 8AM to noon, we had a sales training meeting. We learned
the science of selling from all the available sources. Tapes, books, movies,
and lectures. Every sales expert was played, and replayed – gleaned for
information. None had all. All had some. Napoleon Hill's *Think and Grow
Rich* was mandatory reading and we dissected the book line by line.
Attitude and sales skills became my life.

My friends thought I was nuts – some still do. I watched a Glenn Turner movie (no video in those days), *Challenge to America*, 200 times. It was the best sales pitch I'd ever seen. I had the entire presentation and all the stories memorized.

I became a salesman. My first goal was to be the best salesman in the world. I'm still on that journey, every day.

I started a t-shirt factory with Duke Daulton and Bud Massey in Florida. It was so successful that the title of president was vacated, and we were all vying for the titles of emperor and king. We lost that business because everything we did we measured – who did what and how much. I vowed I would never measure or keep score again. And I haven't. Duke and I went on to become consulting legends (in our own minds), and we had a blast.

After thousands of sales presentations to every conceivable prospect, from Fortune 500 company presidents to unemployed job seekers, and after several huge successes and huge failures in business, I somehow landed in Charlotte, North Carolina, starting over.

My first challenge was to learn how to calm down. I had to adapt the high-speed New York (actually, Philadelphia) style to the pace of this genteel Southern city. That took six months. During that time, I met Joan Zimmerman, a world-class entrepreneur. She said, "Charlotte is a city that you can affect." WOW! What a powerful statement. I decided to stay.

My weekly column *Sales Moves* changed my life. It gave me a vehicle to share my sales knowledge and secrets. I've been writing every week for 15 years. It helped create my brand. It also helped me launch my e-mail magazine *Sales Caffeine* which now has a distribution of more than 300,000 people. More than that, my entire body of work helps me as I formulate the books I write. It give me both content and spurs new thinking and new ideas as I review what was, in order to figure out what is and what will be. The definitive four words about writing are *writing leads to wealth*.

My father, Max – in heaven – taught me to write. He taught me a thousand other things by setting both good and bad examples, but the way he wrote always had my admiration. No wasted words. Absolute clarity of message.

Max was the consummate entrepreneur. Growing up, I used to sneak downstairs and listen to my father's Thursday night pinochle game. Arguments and laughs about business and life. It was the inspiration for my life's pursuits. My pal, Duke Daulton, said, "You know what I hate about your old man? He's never wrong."

I'm grateful to my father for his wisdom – the stuff he accused me of never listening to for 30+ years. Thanks, Pop. I love you. I miss my mother and father.

My brother, Josh, taught me to edit my writing. He has the sensitivity to know how words fit, and the gift to teach it. He showed me where unnecessary words made my writing confusing – and that removing those words increased the clarity of my message 100%.

My children, Erika, Stacey, and Rebecca have taught me patience. They also gave me the inspiration to achieve in the face of failure. Girls, I love you.

My grandchildren, Morgan, Julia, Claudia, and Isabel have rekindled my understanding of unconditional love and unlimited budgets.

The first writing of *The Sales Bible* came at a time when my life was in renaissance. Without going into detail, let me just say that I was hurting – physically, mentally, and financially. When times like this occur, resilience and rebound can only come from attitude.

My attitude was there with my when I was alone. So was my cat, Lito.

Since I first wrote *The Sales Bible*, I've grown up an additional 15 years. And I've learned the subtle difference between growing up and growing old.

I've been fortunate to attract people into my life that have made far more than an impact and a difference. Reuniting with my brother, Josh, who is now an integral part of my business and finding, finally finding, a real friend and partner that I can talk to, be truthful with, travel with, and edit with has created a remarkable difference in my thinking and my life. Jessica McDougall is a brilliant young woman with an old soul and I'm grateful for her friendship and her help.

My objective is to help others, do what I love, establish long-term relationships, and have fun – every day.

Your past and present hold the key to your future.

Where are you going?

No, I don't mean where are you going on your next appointment. I don't mean where are you going out to dinner. And I don't mean where are you going when you get to the mall.

I'm asking: Where are you going in life? That's a pretty big question because *it's about your future.*

Did you miss your quota last month? Last year? How come? Blaming it on the economy again? Blaming it on the competition again? What is a quota anyway? A quota is a goal that *someone else* sets for you. I'm asking: What have you set for yourself? When someone gives you a quota, why not double it? That way you'll make the number with ease. It's all in how you look at things.

GUESS WHAT? You create barriers or you jump over them.

Once a year I try to predict the future. I do it on the anniversary of the beginning of my writing career. This year will mark my seventeenth anniversary. It's always a cause for deep reflection because writing and being published is the fulcrum point of my success.

It's not only about how I've made a name for myself, it's also about the legacy that I will leave salespeople worldwide – and, of course, my children and grandchildren.

Writing is about more than creating new sales information each week that salespeople like you can benefit from. It's about being self-disciplined so I can clarify my own ideas, which form the basis for the speeches that I give and the books that I write.

If you really want to know where you're going, you have to understand where you've been and recognize where you are. Where you've been, or the past, provides you with knowledge and experiences, successes and failures, as well as opportunities and obstacles. Where you are, or the present, is what happened during the past 30 days, what's happening today, as well as what's going to happen within the next 30 days. Where you'll be, or the future, is a combination of your experience, your being open to opportunity, your goals and dreams, your tolerance for risk, as well as your determination and focus.

Let me clarify that and break it down into 3.5 easy-to-digest categories:

1. **Once was.**
2. **As is.**
3. **Can be.**
3.5 **Become.**

Once was is the history of your life. It's the sum total of your knowledge, your wisdom, your experience, your victories, and your defeats. If you look closely at the history of your life, you can see some things that you wanted with all your heart but you didn't get. At the time you were devastated, but in retrospect it seems silly that you ever wanted those things. You can also see some things that you were given or that you earned, but once you got them, you quickly lost interest. More important, you see the things you loved and how they have affected you. You look at the risks you took and think that if you had the opportunity to take them again, you might not. And all of that brings you to *as is*.

As is is where you are today. Are you where you want to be? Are you happy with your lot in life? Are you blaming your lack of success on someone else? Have you found what you are looking for? Do you even know what it is?

Some of us haven't found what we are looking for, but that doesn't mean to stop looking. I didn't start writing until I was forty-five years old. If you're younger than that and you start writing tomorrow, in 13 years you'll be ahead of me.

I'm teaching my granddaughter to write. She'll be 50 years ahead of me.

As is provides you with your greatest single opportunity. It's about how you decide to invest your time and money. The time to take action is now. The time to risk is now. The time to go for what you want is now. The time to educate yourself and study is now. If you do, you may be able to achieve the success you are looking for later.

Many people think that once they're done with high school or college, they're essentially done studying. That may be OK if your closing question is: Will that be paper or plastic?

Success doesn't just show up in the now. Success comes as a result of hard work and focus in the now. But that elusive brass ring you are looking for lies within. It's the *can be*.

Can be is full of dreams, full of goals, and full of serendipity. Some things are not goals. Some things just evolve. And in that evolution, you can find what you really love. If you love something, you don't have to make it a goal. Instead, you just work your butt off, and it becomes reality.

What you can be is going to be a result of your hard work, your positive attitude, your passion, your focus on achievement, and your drive to not let little things stand in your way – even if it means risking what you've got.

Many people in their struggle will come to me and say, "Jeffrey, you don't understand." And then they go on to say something about their personal situation, their money, their spouse, or their kids.

I understand fine. People are afraid to risk what they have in order to go for what they really want. The worst part of not risking is lamenting. Lamenting that you didn't try it, that you didn't go for it, or that you should have done it.

Maybe it's time to read or watch *The Wizard of Oz* again and see how it relates to your life. Remember what Dorothy's companions were searching for? Courage, brains, and heart. You've always known the formula – you just haven't used it. And with very few exceptions, you're not in Kansas anymore.

<blockquote>

And when you combine once was, as is, and can be, the sum of that is what you will become.

</blockquote>

One of the most valuable lessons I have ever learned was from a friend, Dr. Paul Homoly, who said to me, "Make all decisions based on the person you would like to become." That wisdom is so powerful that I think of it everyday. It's been a big part of my success. Perhaps you can use it in your quest to be your best.

Let me throw some words at you. Educate yourself, try your best, risk failure, seize the opportunity, develop self-discipline, dedicate yourself to becoming a winner, and make a commitment that it's for you first and everybody else second.

It's not a formula – it's a philosophy. And philosophy is the secret to getting you from where you are to where you want to be.

I wish you a safe, fun, successful journey. Keep me posted.

Do you or your team need MORE SALES NOW?

I'm available for speaking engagements and training programs. To find out more and hire me, call my friendly office at 704-333-1112 or visit my website www.gitomer.com.

I will design and deliver a customized program for your sales force that will have them laughing, learning, and … selling.

I will make my presentation directly applicable to your selling situation. The program is developed for your company, your product, your customers, and the objections you face in your selling environment.

Your team can take my material out to their prospects and use it to make sales the same day they hear it.

TRAIN YOURSELF: You are also entitled to a free TrainOne sales program. Go to www.trainone.com to view the demo. You need to have high-speed Internet access to view the demo and to become a TrainOne.com subscriber. If you don't, your competition is already beating you.

It's not just cost-effective, it's sales-effective. And it's fun.

A friendly person from my office is standing by at 704.333.1112.

FOUR MILLION READERS OF "SALES MOVES:" If my column is not in your local business paper, call them up and say, "Hey, get Gitomer. Publish his weekly column, 'Sales Moves.' It's helping salespeople all over the country. Get him now!" You are my field sales force. I need your help to achieve my goal of 10 million readers a week by the end of this decade.

www.YANICKDERY.com

Jeffrey Gitomer
Chief Executive Salesman

AUTHOR. Jeffrey Gitomer is the author of The New York Times best sellers *The Sales Bible, The Little Red Book of Selling, The Little Black Book of Connections,* and *The Little Gold Book of YES! Attitude.* All of his books have been number one best sellers on Amazon.com, including *Customer Satisfaction is Worthless, Customer Loyalty is Priceless, The Patterson Principles of Selling, The Little Red Book of Sales Answers,* and his latest best selling book *The Little Green Book of Getting Your Way.* Jeffrey's books have sold millions of copies worldwide.

OVER 100 PRESENTATIONS A YEAR. Jeffrey gives public and corporate seminars, runs annual sales meetings, and conducts live and Internet training programs on selling, customer loyalty, and personal development.

BIG CORPORATE CUSTOMERS. Jeffrey's customers include Coca-Cola, D.R. Horton, Caterpillar, BMW, Cingular Wireless, MacGregor Golf, Ferguson Enterprises, Kimpton Hotels, Hilton, Enterprise Rent-A-Car, AmeriPride, NCR, Stewart Title, Comcast Cable, Time Warner Cable, Liberty Mutual Insurance, Principal Financial Group, Wells Fargo Bank, Baptist Health Care, BlueCross BlueShield, Carlsberg, Wausau Insurance, Northwestern Mutual, MetLife, Sports Authority, GlaxoSmithKline, AC Neilsen, IBM, The New York Post, and hundreds of others.

IN FRONT OF MILLIONS OF READERS EVERY WEEK. Jeffrey's syndicated column Sales Moves appears in scores of business journals and newspapers in the Unted States and Europe, and is read by more than four million people every week.

SELLING POWER LIVE. Jeffrey is the host and commentator of Selling Power Live, a monthly, subscription-based sales resource bringing together the insights of the world's foremost authorities on selling and personal development.

ON THE INTERNET. Jeffrey's WOW! websites, www.gitomer.com and www.trainone.com, get more than 100,000 hits per week from readers and seminar attendees. His state-of-the-art presence on the web and e-commerce ability has set the standard among peers, and has won huge praise and acceptance from his customers.

TRAINONE ONLINE SALES TRAINING. Online sales training lessons are available at www.trainone.com. The content is pure Jeffrey – fun, pragmatic, real world – and can be immediately implemented. TrainOne's innovation is leading the way in the field of customized e-learning.

SALES CAFFEINE. Jeffrey's weekly e-zine, Sales Caffeine, is a sales wake-up call delivered every Tuesday morning to more than 250,000 subscribers, free of charge. Sales Caffeine allows Jeffrey to communicate valuable sales information, strategies, and answers to sales professionals on a timely basis. Get full information at www.salescaffeine.com.

SALES ASSESSMENT ONLINE. The world's first customized sales assessment, renamed a "successment," will not only judge your selling skill level in 12 critical areas of sales knowledge, it will give you a diagnostic report that includes 50 mini sales lessons. This amazing sales tool will rate your sales abilities and explain your customized opportunities for sales knowledge growth. This program is aptly named KnowSuccess because you can't know success until you know yourself.

AWARD FOR PRESENTATION EXCELLENCE. In 1997, Jeffrey was awarded the designation of Certified Speaking Professional (CSP) by the National Speakers Association. The CSP award has been given fewer than 500 times in the past 25 years and is the association's highest earned award.

BuyGitomer, Inc. • 310 Arlington Avenue • Loft 329 • Charlotte, N.C. 28203
www.gitomer.com • 704.333.1112 • salesman@gitomer.com

Other titles by Jeffrey Gitomer

THE LITTLE PLATINUM BOOK OF CHA-CHING!
(FT Press, 2007)

THE LITTLE GREEN BOOK OF GETTING YOUR WAY
(FT Press, 2007)

THE LITTLE GOLD BOOK OF YES! ATTITUDE
(FT Press, 2007)

THE LITTLE BLACK BOOK OF CONNECTIONS
(Bard Press, 2006)

THE LITTLE RED BOOK OF SALES ANSWERS
(FT Press, 2006)

THE LITTLE RED BOOK OF SELLING
(Bard Press, 2004)

CUSTOMER SATISFACTION IS WORTHLESS, CUSTOMER LOYALTY IS PRICELESS
(Bard Press, 1998)